HOW NOT TO BE A ROCK STAR

icon
publishing

First published in July 2012.

icon
publishing

Icon Publishing
185a High Street, Ryde
Isle of Wight
PO33 2PN
UK

Cover photograph & Design by Tim Pritchard
Layout & Design by Neil Hague

British Library Cataloguing-in
Publication Data
A catalogue record for this book is
available from the British Library

ISBN 978-0-9559973-9-6

Printed and bound in India by Thomson Press India Ltd

HOW NOT TO BE A ROCK STAR

GARETH ICKE

DEDICATION

"To all my band mates, friends & family.
I will forever be grateful for your support."

G

CONTENTS

CONTENTS

FORWARD

Thanks a lot for buying, stealing, finding, or merely flicking through this book.

I know forewords are normally written by someone else, someone completely disconnected from the book. In my experience it tends to be someone that is slightly more successful than the author in the field that the publication is about. Let's be honest, the foreword is normally just a load of clap trap that blows smoke up the arse of the writer, not because they genuinely believe the book is any good, but because they've been paid rather handsomely to say so.

Well bugger that; I'll write my own. I just want to briefly explain how I came to put finger to keyboard and put this to print.

I have played in bands for years and have since gone solo and had the odd bit of success here and there; not enough to buy a house, but enough to buy a round of beers. That suits me just fine. I never was one for mowing the lawn and tiling the bathroom anyway.

On one of my many solo tours I ended up in a post gig party in Glasgow. I was a bit drunk and conversational as always. People were exchanging stories about their lives and touring experiences. I told a few stories, all of which were about a previous band Kody. I seemed to have quite an audience. A particular story I told about something that happened in Wales seemed to catch people's attention. Jaws dropped and one rather boisterous Scot informed me that there was no way that story could be true, could it?

Once I'd proved the stories validity, I was told by a now slightly less boisterous and more shell shocked Scot that I should write a book; and so I did.

Believe me, I questioned why on Earth I was doing it many times; after all, who wants to read about an unknown bloke that used to be in a band once? If there was a genuine market for that, every

Waterstones would be the size of Heathrow Terminal 5.

But then I got thinking about a line I used to hear a lot as a kid. "It's not the winning, it's the taking part that counts". Now while this is an old cliché that has never once been uttered by anyone that has ever won anything, it did make some sense.

Ok, so we never made it big, but we had a damn good go and because we did it with raw passion instead of intelligence, we ended up in scrapes that I bet not many other bands have been faced with. We were drunks with hearts of gold and brains of dry roasted peanuts. This combination supplied the stories you're about to read.

I wonder if Coldplay ever had guns pointed at them outside Downing Street?

I wonder if Muse ever witnessed a brutal murder while hiding behind a farmers wall?

I doubt it.

I really hope you enjoy what you read. It is all 100% true. Often fact is stranger than fiction they say. After writing this, I'm inclined to agree.

Peace. G x

INTRODUCTION

My name is Gareth. I am a musician. Well, I try to be. If you reach the end of this book, you may have a very different opinion of whether I do indeed fit into that category.

First of all, I have a confession to make: I've never written a book before. But what I have done, many times, is sit in bars telling the very stories I'm about to tell you.

So, let's pretend we're sat in a bar – The Dog & Partridge. I don't know why I plucked that name out of the sky, but it seems like a suitable small-English-town name for a pub.

The Dog & Partridge sounds like the kind of place that would still have the same nicotine-stained walls that it had back in the 1970s. It's not clean; but it's homely. It has a jukebox and a pool table, and the locals have names like Sparky, Gunner and Spud. Are you getting a mental image? I hope so.

I sit down next to you at the bar and order a Guinness. We get chatting about the weather, the troubles with "the youth", and then we inevitably get to the "tell me about yourself" bit.

I'm aware that this meeting seems somewhat friendly for an old English boozer; flirtatious even. But just go with it.

I'll give you a bit of background about me and my friends so that the characters in the stories make a lot more sense.

As I said, I'm Gareth. I grew up on the Isle of Wight. For those of you who don't know, it's a small Island about four miles off the south coast of England. It is beautiful, I'll give it that. But for lads in their teens and twenties, there isn't a lot to do. You basically have a choice: drugs and petty crime; become a cog in a very poorly paid machine; or start a punk rock band.

My mates and I went for the latter.

I was born in 1981, so I grew up in the musical era of Nirvana, Pearl Jam, Stone Temple Pilots and the like. I'm pretty grateful for that when I hear what the kids today have as their musical backdrop. Christ – that makes me sound old!

So anyway, the natural thing to do was to start up a punk rock band and try to take over the world. My armada was a band called "Kody". That's the band that all the stories you're about to read are about.

It was formed around 2002, with the sole purpose of making music, drinking shitloads of beer, touring the planet and, one day maybe, making enough money to pay the rent. In the end, we did all but the last part. But three out of four isn't bad for a bunch of idiots from the Isle of Wight.

I formed the band with a couple of fellahs I met down the local pub – much like the way we've just met. Only this local was called The Royal Squadron, and not The Dog & Partridge. "The Squadron" or "The Squaddie" was all we kids had in terms of live music. I'm pretty sure I was a regular part-of-the-furniture drinker in there about three years before I was legally allowed to be. And bearing in mind the legal drinking age in England is 18, that's quite a feat.

If I had to describe The Squadron, I would simply say it was dark. Oh, and it stank of sweat. In fact, if I had thrown a slice of toast onto the ceiling back then, I reckon it would still be there today. You know the sort of place – the best sort of place.

So, the first chap was called Steve Richmond – a good-looking lad and always quite a hit with the ladies. He'd already played bass in other bands so I'd seen him a bunch of times. He'd often wear nail varnish and skirts and whatever else he felt like wearing. But when you're six-foot-odd and you've got some decently-chiselled looks, you can pretty much get away with anything, fashion wise. Back in those days, men that looked like women were a real catch. I never did get the thinking behind that. But I suppose I didn't need to. I'd just whack a bit of eyeliner on and hope for the best.

So, Steve was the bass player and we needed a drummer. Finding a drummer on the Isle of Wight is like finding an honest politician. But somehow we managed it in an incredibly tall lad called Simon Cook.

If I asked you to describe a punk rock drummer, I'd bet you a pint of Guinness that you'd describe the polar opposite of Simon. He was always smartly dressed, came from a rich family and, more strikingly, he was about eight feet tall. He basically looked like a Scandinavian long-distance runner. I mean, I'm over six foot myself and this guy towers over me. But, he was rock 'n' roll through and through. Actually, in hindsight, not looking punk rock made him more punk rock.

I keep saying "punk rock". It's an annoying term, eh?

So, you have a mental image of the band? Well, apart from me. In those days I was as skinny as a rake, wore ripped jeans, and, despite being a hardy drinker (or so I thought), I looked about 12. In fact, to make it easier for the older readers, I looked like a young Oliver Reed.

The band was born. We started off with covers, as all bands do. If Bush, Silverchair or Nirvana had heard what we did to their songs, they'd turn in their graves. Even if they weren't dead, they'd find a grave, climb into it and begin to turn furiously. See, what I've failed to mention in all this reminiscing is we weren't very good. We had all the passion in the world. But not a lot of ability.

I played guitar (badly) and sang. Now I don't know how to describe my voice back then other than to ask you to imagine a guy that's jumped off the Empire State Building and plummeted all the way to the sidewalk below. It's not a pleasant image, I know; but I sang about as flat as that chap would have been. Only with me, you got the added bonus of a fake American accent.

Don't mock me. I'm being honest! All my favourite bands were American. And I couldn't just "be myself" – I was just 18.

So, the flat-singing 12-year-old Oliver Reed, the handsome cross-dresser and Sven Svensson set about world domination. Where best to start than right at home – The Royal Squadron.

The music nights were run by a guy called Dan Damage. This man is, and will always be, a hero on the Isle of Wight music scene. What John Lennon said about Elvis applies here: before him, there was nothing. And for some bizarre reason, he actually liked us. I think he liked us because we didn't give a shit about what people thought. We had the punk attitude, the smashed guitars and the onstage antics; we just didn't have the musical bit. Which matters, apparently. Who'd have thought it?!

So, that was the next step. We were going to be the first band in The Royal Squadron to play our own stuff. After all, none of us was up for being in a tribute band. To us, back then, tribute bands were a form of legal prostitution; only it was your soul you were selling, and not your arse.

I wrote the songs, and we pieced them together. Now, I'll be the first to admit, the songs weren't great – but they were ours. And that was half the battle. We had a set of original songs and now all we needed to do was get better at playing them.

I was never the greatest guitar player and, with me being the sole guitarist in the band, that was kind of a big issue. So we managed, after much persuasion, to get in another guitarist – a girl by the name of Charlotte Ripley.

The fact that we had another guitarist was a good thing, musically; but the fact that she was a girl, and a damn pretty girl too, well, that was awesome. Now we could get the boys to gigs. Even if they didn't like the songs, they liked *her* and they paid a few quid to get in. Everyone's a winner.

I'll admit, I think all three of us lads had a major crush on Charlotte. She was petite, blonde and just oozed rock 'n' roll. Kind of like a Courtney Love only not 12 feet tall, drug addicted or mental.

Things were looking up. The songs were getting better, the band was sounding a lot more like a band, and just generally things were good. But – and there is always a but – if any of you have grown up in a small town, you'll know other people don't always like things being good for you – especially if things aren't going well at *their* end. It says something about them that they don't want to hear. So they pull you down. Or at least they try to.

This was around the time that the Internet became a big thing. Chat rooms and local music forums appeared everywhere, and everyone on the Isle of Wight had something to say about Kody. Almost none of it was positive.

Insults flew around about how arrogant we were, and how Americanised we were, and how we were just a poor man's Bush. Okay, that sounded rude. I meant the band Bush. You know the one – the singer married Gwen Stefani from No Doubt.

Such wonderful insults. They spread from the Internet and ended up at our shows. Some idiots would shout stuff while we were playing, throw beer at the stage, and just generally be a pain in the arse. And while it all sounds very trivial, it was massively important for us and for what the band went on to become; although we didn't think so at the time. Live performances were halted; punches were thrown. You know the drill.

They were right though. We were a bit arrogant. We were teenagers, for crying out loud! Teenagers know it all; we all know that. And yes, we *did* sound American and we *were* a poor man's...

y'know. But what we realised more than anything was that we needed to get off the Isle of Wight. We needed people to take the music at face value. Everyone we were playing to had a preconceived idea about us – before we'd even played an out-of-tune note.

We had done a couple of shows on mainland England – horrible little gigs where you had to move the pool table to set up, and the sound system was no bigger than a karaoke machine. They were pretty depressing shows. So we thought, hey, if we sound American they'll love us in the States.

So, we got some cheap flights to Chicago and flew out. It really was that simple. When we landed, we bought the local Chicago paper and started looking for open mic nights and stuff like that. We were there for two weeks, and we played about ten shows and ended up doing a radio interview as well. I won't tell you any more about that trip as one of the stories later will tell you all you need to know about what went on in the old US of A.

When we returned home, things were different. Charlotte hadn't come out to America and it was pretty clear that she wasn't as into the band as we were. Which is fair enough – it was our baby; we were always going to love it more. So she left, and we went back to being a three-piece.

America was so important to us because what it told us was that anything was possible. We were three small-town English lads and we just flew out to America and rocked out for two weeks. This was no longer a hobby for us – this was a serious band.

All we wanted was for more people to hear our music. So we stopped charging for CDs. We just handed them out to whoever would take a copy. The recordings were done on the cheap, so we weren't really losing money (which was a good thing, as none of us had any – a theme that would continue for the entire life of the band).

It was around this time that the three of us moved in together. Now, they say that living together is the biggest test of a relationship; and they aren't lying. Not least for Steve and Simon. These guys had been all the way through school together, they'd worked behind the bar at the Squadron together (although I'm sure they spent most of their time trying to get me drunk when I was meant to be DJing), but living together was a step too far. Arguments began, and got more and more frequent and more and more aggressive; then in the end it all blew up with a punch-up in the kitchen. Simon packed his stuff and left the band. I hadn't seen that coming.

Back to square one, then – just Steve and me. As I mentioned before, drummers don't exist on the Isle of Wight. It's almost like a practical joke that has gone on for generations. If you show promise as a drummer when you're a kid, you can bet that you'll be losing those fingers in some kind of heavy-machinery accident before you reach adulthood.

I did know one drummer ... a character named Turlough. We had a love–hate relationship in those days though. I think he thought I was a bit of a dick and I thought he was a little bit mental. Turns out we were both dicks and we were both a little bit mental. Match made in heaven. We'd known each other since we were little. That's the Isle of Wight all over – everyone knows everyone; something that can be both a blessing and a curse.

Turlough was probably the single biggest catalyst in the band's history. His presence was immense. There is an aura about him that just makes you want to be around him. He brings out the best in people; and he certainly did that with me and Steve.

Turlough Ducie is one hell of a rock star name, right? Well, he looked every bit the rock star too; a proper 1970s American rock star. The kind that could play a show, get arrested, get deported, and still find time to sleep with a female police officer. He was a massive, hairy bloke, and Christ did he smash those drums.

Every song we had immediately became louder and bigger and more "in your face". If people hadn't taken notice of us before, they had to now.

With all positives often comes a negative though. It's the way life goes. The only negative that Turlough brought was that he worked in a pub – a place called The Solent Inn. It's still my local to this day. It's a lot more upmarket now, but in those days it was the Dog & Partridge. In fact, Sparky and Gunner actually drank in there.

Steve and I – very innocently I must add – ended up spending a lot more time in the pub, and it started a downward spiral that lead to some of the things you'll read about later on. So I won't give too much away – this is only an introduction after all.

Another thing that Turlough brought to the table was his group of friends. It's the Isle of Wight, so we all knew each other to say "All right?" to in the street, but not a lot more than that. All of his mates were musicians of one sort or another, and we were still lacking that second guitarist and backing vocalist. I'd always sung on my own, but we needed someone else for choruses and harmonics to bulk us up, especially as we now had a drummer that was such a big hitter.

One of the guys we knocked about with was Tim Pritchard. I always thought he was an annoying little bloke who made it his life's mission to wind me up. He succeeded several times, but I suppose I was pretty annoying too. He used to be the frontman of a heavy metal band called "Igor". Actually, a few years before, Steve and I had asked Tim if he would support us, and when he said, "Yeah, sure", we put our entire bodyweight on each of his shoulders.

Okay, so we were all just as annoying as each other.

Tim was a good-looking lad. Not as tall as the rest of us, but he was younger, so those boyish good looks were still firmly in place – for now.

Tim was a great guitarist and his voice was a perfect accompaniment to my own. His was a lot higher than mine but the two harmonised well. Tim had a mental stage presence, despite having asthma, and he would play a back-end boozer like it was Wembley Stadium.

With the addition of Turlough and Tim, the band had just trebled in quality. Scrap that and multiply it by a hundred! Within a month, everyone's perception had changed. Kody could actually play a bit – thanks in no short measure to having a rehearsal space for the first time. That was another thing that came wrapped up in the Tim Pritchard parcel – an outhouse that we could rehearse in seven days a week.

So, that's what we did. Every single day we were locked in that room playing over and over and over. It did get boring after a while, but, once we felt the results, it was worth it. People were actually listening to us. The local radio station was playing our demos, and the local newspaper was printing stories about our shows. We'd landed. Sort of. We were just one step away from becoming a professional band.

None of us had a clue about the business side of things. We just wanted to make a noise and sink some beers and hope the rest would take care of itself. It doesn't work like that, unfortunately, and so we needed someone who knew all that stuff. We needed a manager.

A local businessman by the name of James had taken an interest in what we were up to. He was well known around the Island but no-one really knew what he did or how he made his money. He owned a bar or two, and maybe a few properties, but no-one really had a clue where this wealth had come from. People came up with underworld criminal conspiracies about him. It's a small island, so gossip is par for the course; but what people say about someone, and what are the actual facts, tend to be very different things. We treated as we found and he was always decent enough to us.

He was a short, balding bloke, about 38, and he always wore dodgy floral shirts. But despite this, he always had an attractive girl on his arm. Maybe this is where the tales of illegal activity came from. Jealousy is a terrible thing.

So, we arranged a meeting in a local wine bar and we had a chat. He was quite a charmer, and the effects of the champagne didn't take too long to kick in. Here we were, the four of us sat around a table drinking expensive bubbly with the local Alan Sugar/Al Capone (depending on who you believed), agreeing for him to take charge of the band.

The first thing James did was bring in another member. Now, as you can imagine, this didn't go down amazingly well. We were a tight-knit family unit until now. Steve and I still lived together, and Turlough and Tim lived in the next street. The last thing we needed was an outsider to come in and screw up the balance of stuff. But he was the manager, and for once I thought I'd keep my mouth shut and see what happened.

The new guy was called Dan Hill and he was a DJ. I'd seen his posters up around the Island. He'd play hip-hop nights and stuff like that. I didn't really get what he was going to bring to the band. We were a rock band – not Sublime.

I'm not the first to admit when I'm wrong, but I will admit it eventually. In the case of Dan Hill, I was wrong. He fitted in perfectly, and within 10 minutes we were hanging out like we'd been the best of mates for years. He did a bit of scratching over a few songs, but, more importantly, he played the keyboard. In a short time we'd gone from a noisy three-piece to a melodic, piano-laced five-piece. Hands up, James – you got it right.

During this whole time, Steve and I were struggling financially. Simon had left the house and with him his share of the rent. We'd been making up the deficit barely and we really needed a permanent lodger to move in. Dan lived in Ventnor which is about nine miles from where we all lived in Ryde. Getting to rehearsals was becoming difficult for him, so he moved in with me and Steve. Perfect.

Dan Hill was a funny guy. Good looking and really skinny. In fact, his chest had a massive dent in it. I've never seen a man go inwards before. I once watched him lying on his back eating cornflakes out of the cave in his chest. You don't easily recover from watching something like that.

The five of us set about – under the wing of our manager, James – taking over the Isle of Wight. We wanted to really crack it there before we moved on to try to break London. And we succeeded with the help of some illegal advertising techniques. You'll read about that later.

We'd booked up a couple of shows on the southwest coast of mainland England. We were playing in Exeter and Plymouth.

I naively thought that our gear and the five of us would fit into Steve's Ford Sierra. It wouldn't. So we had about three days to find a van, and a man to drive it; and not just a

man to drive it, but a man who wouldn't mind being away from work for two days while not getting paid by us because we weren't getting paid ourselves!

The van bit was sorted pretty quickly. A local chap in the Solent Inn called Tuckey overheard our despair and lent us his.

"Cheers, Tuckey!"

"All right."

That's the amazing thing about local pubs like the Solent Inn and the Dog & Partridge – the level of trust. I'm not sure I'd just chuck five drunken lads the keys to my car. Well, unless they were wielding knives.

We now had the van but not the man.

There was a Welsh guy that came into the Solent occasionally. We never really spoke to him that much because, to be honest, his fiancé did all the talking you could possibly want. If you'd climbed Everest, she'd done it walking backwards in her Flip Flops. You know the sort.

But he said, "I'll drive you."

I didn't even know this guy's name, and here he was offering to be in charge of getting us to and from two very important shows. Hell, beggars can't be choosers and we didn't have a lot of choice.

The unnamed Welshman turned out to be one of the biggest and most significant things to happen to Kody. He was a legend. Now, I know that word is flung about a fair bit – but this guy was the real deal.

Nigel Lloyd was a proper Welsh Valleys' lad. He was about 40, covered in tattoos, and he made Tim look tall. He was christened Taffy (an unimaginative nickname for a Welshman, I know) and he was family member number six.

For the next few years he would drive us everywhere, set up the gear, cook us meals, and so on. He became our father on tour.

I'll take a few seconds to give you a brief bit of background on Taffy. He'll be a pretty important character in nearly all the stories you're about to – hopefully – enjoy.

Taff had grown up in Aberdare, South Wales – a small coal-mining town that was completely destroyed by the Conservative Party in the 1980s. It closed the mines and closed the doors on the people's livelihood – all without any remorse or thought for their survival.

Taff was a product of this town. With virtually zero employment, he ended up joining the Army, where, after a while, he smacked his superior and ended up getting thrown

out. After getting into trouble with the police in Wales, he moved to England, met the woman that talked a lot, and ended up on the Isle of Wight and in my local pub.

Hopefully you have a mental image of Taffy, and an idea of his character.

After a few more shows we parted company with James, and, a little while later, with Dan Hill. It had worked for a while but, in the end, Dan wanted to go back to his hip-hop stuff, and James was too busy with his business projects.

We honestly felt at the time that it was better for us to do it on our own anyway. We felt we'd learned enough in the last few months and we'd pick up the rest as we went along. We weren't going to be one of those bands that got picked up at a competition or sent demos to thousands of labels. We were going to be a band that got in a van and toured. Then, when we'd stopped touring, we'd tour some more.

What we didn't have was a van. And, more importantly, we didn't have the money to buy one.

Cue Sparky Brian. Brian was another Solent Inn local. He was, as his name suggests, an electrician. What he'd also done, apparently, was some technical stuff for Dexy's Midnight Runners. You remember them, right? Well if you don't, you'll remember the song *Come on Eileen* – an absolute classic that's always played at weddings. Well, unless the bride is called Eileen and then you'd perhaps want to skip that one on the playlist.

I'm rambling.

Sparky was basically a top bloke – a real nice guy who loved his music and loved his booze; much like ourselves. He offered to lend us £2000 to buy a van – which was an incredible gesture from even a rich man, let alone a humble sparky. I told you our local pub was awesome, didn't I?

So, armed with our two grand, we went on the search for a van. We found a few that were okay. Needed plenty of work though and with only £2000 in our pocket, we couldn't afford a mechanical "project".

Just when we'd pretty much given up hope, we saw an advert for a bus for sale. It was AMAZING! Far too rich for our blood though. It was a Ford Transit that hadn't done many miles, and it was owned by Age Concern (now Age UK). Age UK is a charity that looks after elderly people. It will take them to hospital appointments for instance when they have no transport. So, it was pretty obvious that the engine hadn't been abused too much. You can't risk taking corners too fast with old people in the back. There would have been hips cracking all over the place!

So, we went to Age Concern and made them an offer. Two grand was all we had so it was all we offered. And they accepted! Madness! We'd got really lucky there, and the lady in charge, Alison, admitted that they'd had a better offer but that the idea of it going to help some young lads make it in the music industry had made them all really excited. How cool is that?

So we took the van, named it after Alison, and the band was complete.

We embarked on a massive tour – 28 shows in 28 days from one end of England to the other. It was named the *You Have* tour and was our first proper taste of life on the road. No hotels or anything – just sleeping bags and a van.

Again, I won't say too much as a couple of the stories later on are about this tour. What I will do though is explain the tour's name.

If we were out having a beer for instance and we saw someone we didn't particularly like or get along with, we used to say, "You've got him written all over you." The problem is, people would often hear us and that could be awkward. Also, if we saw someone walking down the street that, say, stank of urine, you couldn't exactly say,

"Look at that bloke. Can you smell him? That's piss." People don't take kindly to that. So, we developed a "You have".

"You have" basically means: Look around you, there is something slightly amusing or weird taking place.

The reason we named the tour after this saying? I have no idea. But that's the meaning, anyway.

After a few days on the tour, I got a call from a guy called Gary. He had heard some of the band's tunes and was interested in helping us out in a managerial capacity. I don't think Gary had ever managed a band before but he was enthusiastic and was willing to invest money in us. That was something we desperately needed. We needed some decent recordings, too, for a start. I mean, when you're bumming around on your island you can get away with dodgy home recordings; but we were playing out of our comfort zones now and the audiences expected a lot more from us.

We met up with Gary just outside London, had a drink and agreed that we'd work together and we'd get some decent recordings done when we got back from the tour. Everything was starting to take shape for us. We had the line-up sorted, we had Taffy at the helm of our new touring wagon, and it appeared that we were about to have a manager with funds to take us to the next level.

Needless to say, the atmosphere on the tour was one of excitement. We really thought this was the start of something. And in many ways it was.

But, like in all things, every positive has a negative to wrestle with. Steve was starting to struggle on the tour. It was bloody hard work, and with the lack of sleep, lack of good food and overall lack of finances, it did take its toll – on all of us.

I think it affected Steve a lot more because he'd recently fallen in love. It's sounds cheesy, but it's true. We were all skint and we were all tired but Steve was really missing his girlfriend and I honestly think that despite being in a vanful of lads, he was lonely. I can relate to that though. You can feel at your most alone when you're in a crowd of people.

It was different for the rest of us. This tour was more like an escape – especially for me and Taffy. Taffy had recently split up from the woman that talked a lot; as for me, my girlfriend had gone to Spain for a few months and I was missing her terribly. But being at home and seeing her stuff all around and seeing her family and friends was harder than being out on the road. So, I guess Taffy and I were feeling the complete opposite to how Steve felt.

Three weeks into the tour, Steve finally snapped. He really couldn't cope with it, and it was horrible for me to see my friend this unhappy. His performances suffered and he started making more and more mistakes on stage. I could understand that completely though. His mind was elsewhere – tucked up in a nice warm bed with his girlfriend where he didn't have to worry about money, and where he didn't have to listen to me and Turlough giggling like schoolchildren in our double sleeping-bag.

It finally came to a head. We sat around a table and thrashed it out. It wasn't working and the atmosphere was unbearable. Steve left the band and went back to the Isle of Wight.

I remember that conversation like it was yesterday. I was completely gutted. Steve and I had formed this band and I honestly thought we'd go the whole way together. All I wanted from that conversation was for Steve to say he'd deal with his issues and sort his head out. None of us wanted him to leave the band and I know that Turlough certainly felt the same as I did. Why hadn't Steve fought for his place? That had confused all of us. He was meant to say he'd try harder. Then, we'd have sorted it out and carried on like nothing had happened. That was the script, wasn't it? Instead, we were driving down to a show in Brighton that afternoon without a bass player. Little did we know that the bass-player position would be vacated far too many times over the next few years.

Turlough's younger brother, Ollie, was a cracking musician and could pretty much turn his hand to anything. He was our saviour. We picked him up from the Isle of Wight ferry terminal in Portsmouth and he learned the songs on the hour-long drive along the coast to Brighton.

When we arrived at the venue, they'd double-booked us. We were basically given the option of a 15-minute set to nobody at the start of the night, or no show at all.

We were never ones to turn down a set, no matter how short; but in this case we did. It meant my throat could have a rest and Ollie would have another day to get the songs sorted before we headed to London for the final show of the tour.

We loaded the van with booze and drove about half an hour out of Brighton to find a lay-by to sleep in. We had The Half Moon in Putney the following night and we needed sleep. We actually ended up in a country pub where a bloke kept buying us drinks and we ended up sleeping in the car park. So much for the big show preparation.

If you haven't heard of the Half Moon, it is one of London's most famous live-music venues. Many huge names have played there, including the Rolling Stones, U2 and The Who. And while none of us could stand U2, it was still a pretty impressive band-name to have shared a stage with.

(Just to clarify, I don't mind U2's music – I just can't stand Bono. Never trust a man that wears sunglasses indoors and refers to himself as a rock star without a drop of irony.)

We were already in London by the time we'd all woken up. Taffy was on Army-time and so was always up and awake at stupid o'clock in the morning. He'd woken up and driven us into town before we'd even realised.

The first thing Turlough did was stumble out of the bus and vomit down the side of the Half Moon itself. He'd taken to doing this a lot lately. I must admit though, as far as passers-by were concerned, it was pretty rock 'n' roll.

None of us had shaved for our whole month away. And to make our physical appearance worse, we were drinking like proverbial fish. For every beer you drank, you had to make a notch on the beer count. It didn't matter whether it was a beer, a whisky or a glass of wine – it was one notch. At the end of the tour, you added up the notches and divided by 28 (the number of days we were away). My daily average was 9.6. So over a 28-day period, that's 269 drinks. I'll say that again: that's 269 alcoholic drinks passing down my throat. Wow!

We were one big fat hungover bearded mess. Well, all apart from Taffy who had fashioned a handlebar moustache. It looked so bad, it looked amazing! We were officially a rock band now.

The show went really well despite the vomit, beards and Ollie's lack of rehearsing. What made the night even better was that my then-girlfriend flew back early to surprise me. I don't know why that's important and why I shared that with you. Nice thing to do though, right?

After that tour, it was hard adjusting to life back on the Island. You know when you get something amazing, it's great at first but then you get used to it after a while. That can be pretty dangerous. We were used to being surrounded by strangers telling us how great we were. Now we were back on our island where no-one was a stranger and everyone was pretty aware that we weren't great.

I think Turlough and I struggled most, and we found ourselves slipping deeper and deeper into the pub's clutches and into the booze.

It was around this time we had a complete epiphany. The Solent Inn is a pub divided into two rooms. The bar is in the middle and serves the two. We always sat at the bar in the Spithead Lounge. It's the smaller bar but it was cosier and it had the TV in it so we could watch the football results. From our seats we could look across the bar and see the folks sitting in the other lounge. One afternoon, the other bar comprised the usual clientele of Sparky Brian, Tuckey and Ted. This was a group of blokes linked more through beer than actual friendship. Turlough and I were chatting about the people in the pub, and I said, "How do they afford it? They're in here as soon as it opens, up until it closes, seven days a week. Whatever hour of the day, they're in here, sat at that bar."

Now for the life of me I can't remember who said it, but someone just looked at me and said, "How do you know?"

"Eh?"

"Well how would you know that they're in here everyday, unless you were here to see them?"

Wow! That was a wake-up call if ever I'd had one.

We needed to get back on the road and start playing again. We needed something positive to happen because we'd reached a peak after the *You Have* tour and then it had started to fade away.

I've found that many times in life when you most need a lift or when you're most near to the edge of the cliff, something will come along and give you the boost you need. That boost was a man named Nick Smith.

Nick was a top producer who had worked with some massive names, including Sting and Pink Floyd. He knew his stuff and he'd taken a liking to us. Our new manager, Gary, had been very quiet, and as far as we were concerned he'd lost interest. It turns out that he was quietly going about his business and getting the name "Kody" mentioned around some pretty influential people. Nick was one of those people and he was really eager to record us.

We were an experiment at this point, so the decision was made to record a four-track EP first. If this worked, we'd look at making an album.

I got along really well with Nick. He was a slight man and he looked nothing like we expected. There is usually an air of arrogance around anyone in the music industry and

he simply didn't have it. He looked just like a bloke that you'd find down your local greyhound track – a proper Londoner, a salt-of-the-earth type.

Before we started recording, he would phone me just for a chat. I'd never experienced this before. All I thought a producer was, in my experience, was a man that pressed "record" and then "stop". But Nick was different. He wanted to know how I ticked as a frontman and as a songwriter. What was my motivation? Then, once he knew who and what I was, he could produce the songs in a way that would reflect that.

I don't think Nick had banked on me being such a maniac though. My relationship with my girlfriend was on the rocks, in no small part down to my constant drinking, and I was basically a bit lost. Nick had gone from record producer to Samaritan.

The van was loaded up and we were off to Surrey to make our first proper CD. The studio was part-owned by Chesney Hawkes. You remember? "I am the one and only! Nobody I'd rather be." What a song! A one-hit wonder, but what an amazing one-hit wonder!

We set about recording the *Walking With Lucy* EP. Four tracks in two days, including mixing. It was tight, but we'd managed it and Nick had really captured the sound we wanted. It was rocky and not too polished; much like us as people.

The other thing we managed to get out of this recording was Chesney Hawkes' phone number. Though I'm pretty sure he changed it after we got drunk and called him in the middle of the night.

"Chesney ... come to a party, mate! We've got beer and YOU ARE THE ONE AND ONLY!!!!"

Phone hung up.

So, we headed back to the Isle of Wight, positive, and most importantly of all armed with a top-quality recording.

Our local radio station had played our songs before, but now it was blasting the songs out all the time. Our local HMV record store took our CD and we outsold every other single for one day only.

Kody was on the map; albeit a local map – but a map, nonetheless.

It came to the point very soon when we were in London for shows every week, sometimes driving up on a Wednesday and then again on the Saturday. They were good shows like The Marquee Club and The Barfly – but they weren't paying. There's that whole thing in

London where they think you should feel privileged just to be playing there.

Obviously, making the hour-long boat trip and the two-hour drive twice a week wasn't sustainable, especially as we weren't getting paid for shows.

Gary made the decision to get us all up to London permanently. To be honest, it wasn't really what we wanted. We were an Isle of Wight band. We didn't want to become just another London outfit. But logistically it did make sense.

We relocated to a place called East Molesey. It's a five-minute walk to Hampton Court and Richmond. It was posh, basically. Far too posh for a load of bearded boozepots like us! We stayed in the house of a guy called Lance for a couple of months. Lance was a mate of Gary's and was an all-round nice bloke. He was obsessed with The Who. All over the house were memorabilia and posters. He owned his own business and was doing pretty well for himself; but at heart he was a rocker.

Lance was about forty. Didn't look it and certainly didn't act it. He was a good-looking chap; olive skinned, confident, and popular with the ladies. He liked his booze, too, so he fitted right in with us.

I won't tell you any more than the fact that we were five lads in one room, drinking and gigging all the time. There was some carnage. You'll read about that later.

So things continued to go well for us in London, and Gary decided it was time to record a full album. There was just the small issue of finding the extra investment. Gary had funded the EP, but albums cost the big bucks!

We'd been out and about and people had displayed an interest in investing. But what I've learned is never to trust anyone to do something until they've actually done it. A few broken promises and unreturned calls later and we found our man.

Kody had been doing stupidly well in a Covent Garden "Battle of the Bands". Now let me explain: we all *hated* the idea of competing musicians, but we were entered; and as far as we were concerned, we were playing to a packed venue of strangers that had never heard us before. We certainly didn't expect to keep winning rounds and keep progressing. But it happened, and with it came more interest. A businessman called Mike just happened to be on a night out when he stumbled upon the venue. Mike was the best kind of businessman – the kind that works hard for the sole purpose of playing extremely hard when 5 pm comes. He liked rock 'n' roll, and women, and anything else that was potentially bad for him. He sported the unbuttoned shirt / hairy chest and jeans look – the kind of image you can't pull off unless you're minted.

We played our set and he came over to say he thought it was cool. Musicians get that a lot whether the gig was good or not. It's just a throwaway line that you say to bands if you've accidentally made eye contact with them. Turns out the guy came from Shanklin – a town about seven miles from us on the Isle of Wight! Connection was made, and after a few days of subtle persuasion from Gary the money was invested and we were off to make our first album.

There is something of a bond between small-town folk. I'm sure it's an "us against the world" attitude. Mike obviously wanted us to succeed, and I guess he must have thought we would.

The studio was all booked up through the producer, Nick Smith. He'd done a great job on the last recording and he already knew how we worked and how I ticked as a human being.

We recorded at a place called Parkgate Studios – a huge complex just outside the town of Battle in East Sussex. You've heard of the Battle of Hastings in 1066? William the Conqueror, and all that? Well, that's where we recorded, right smack bang in the middle of where that took place.

It was unbelievable! The place had tonnes of en-suite bedrooms, and a games room with pool tables and PlayStation consoles. We even had our own chef that cooked us whatever we wanted. It was crazy! We were being treated like kings and we hadn't even strummed a chord yet.

The minute we walked into the studio itself, we felt we'd landed. The mixing desk was about the size of my house on the Isle of Wight, and the room we recorded in was probably about the size of the Isle of Wight itself.

How had we managed to get here? It was surreal. From having hecklers at half-empty shows to recording at one of the top studios in the UK and being treated like royalty. I'm not sure my mind could cope with it, to be honest.

Because we didn't have a whole lot of money, and the money we *did* have wasn't ours, recording was a nightmare. Fifteen songs in fifteen days, including mixing and overdubs and everything. By the end I was singing four or five lead vocals a day with backing vocals and double tracking. My throat was ruined. Taffy tried to keep me going with lemon & ginger tea and spoonfuls of honey between takes. It was just delaying the inevitable and, finally, my voice blew out. I simply couldn't sing anymore. In fact, I couldn't even talk. To attempt that many songs in that many days was just plain stupid, and Nick the producer had said so several times. The album was completed and was basically just a fraction of what it could have become.

Occasionally, I'll listen to it and it will really annoy me that we rushed something that could have been great. But such is life. I was never one to moan and so I just got on with it.

The other guys weren't as, shall I say, diplomatic in their opinions of the whole thing. A wedge had formed between the band and the management, and little me was the only thread of cloth still holding the two together.

It was Tim's 21st birthday, and his parents had paid for all of us to go to New York for a week. It was a great chance for everyone to lick their wounds, let the whole album fiasco

die down and get on with pushing the band forward (again, New York will be featured later on so I won't expand too much on it here). But when we returned to London, the wedge between band and management was finally driven home for good.

Okay, so the record wasn't exactly how we'd wanted it; but while in New York we'd tried to focus on the positives. The songs were strong and it didn't sound anything like the music that was in the charts at the time. That was a real plus for us and certainly something to be proud of.

Tim's brother, Ben, had put together some awesome artwork. Ben was a graphic designer and website builder by trade so it was always going to look classy. We told him some rough ideas of what we wanted, and he made it look great.

The album was going to be called *Polaroids From Alison* ("Alison" being the bus, and "Polaroids" being the little snapshots of life we'd seen on the road – the shots that created the ideas for songs and shaped us as a band).

The cover picture was of a brown ploughed-up field with a grey sky. In the middle was a Polaroid, and on it was a bright-green tree and clear blue sky. It looked great, and summed up our feelings about the album itself – seeing the best in a bad situation.

A week or so after we got back, we were playing a show in Leicester Square. We arrived at the venue to be greeted by Gary and

Mike and the finished album. We opened up the box like children open a present on Christmas morning hoping there will be a games console inside it. This was our first album! As soon as we took it out of the box, we all fell silent. It was awful. They'd scrapped all our artwork ideas and instead had put a stretched photo of us sat in a garden on the front. Here I was, the frontman and songwriter, and my head was hidden behind Tim's knees. We just didn't understand what they were thinking. I don't know if we ever actually sold a copy of that album.

That was the final straw between band and management, and within a couple of weeks we'd gone our separate ways. The lads and I were back on the Isle of Wight – homeless, jobless and without management. How quickly things can change in this business.

But, as I said earlier, when you least expect it the best things can happen. We'd met another music manager called Dominic at that Leicester Square gig. Gary had brought him along to pick his brain and generally get some advice about what to do next. Dominic had seen what had gone on with the album and I honestly think he felt sorry for us. Things had been handled wrongly at every stage of the recording process. But Gary wasn't a manager; he was a guy that was trying his best in a cut-throat industry that takes no prisoners. I didn't feel anger towards Gary – I was just disappointed that things had been handled so poorly. As I said before, the rest of the lads were less understanding.

Dominic was at the opposite end of the spectrum to Gary. He didn't care about us as people. He was a professional manager, and in his mind his job was to manage – not

befriend. One of his first lines to me was, "Cut your hair, mate. You look like a footballer."

"I am a footballer."

He was right. The image was all wrong and really didn't suit the music we were playing. We looked like a metal band and sounded like an indie band. He sorted the style and also put us in the studio with another top producer. This time, it was for just two songs; recorded properly, and not rushed.

We recorded in a studio in Hoxton Square, London, with a producer called Simon Hanhart. I won't give too much away about this recording session but let me just say, we were in London in July 2005. Bombs were going off and we ended up just a little too close to the situation.

The recording itself came out great, but the rifts between band and management had spread and were now between ourselves. We'd lived in each other's pockets for a very long time and it had taken its toll on all of us.

Emotionally, we were drained. We'd all sacrificed so much to be part of this band and now the weight of what we had given up was dragging us down.

The band was on borrowed time, and within just a few months Dominic had walked away, the bass player, Ollie, had quit, and things were falling apart.

Tim, Turlough and I had decided to give it one more push. We barely had the energy to, but we figured that we'd worked so hard over the years to make this band great, that we owed it to ourselves to give it one more big drive.

Ollie was replaced by a local Island musician called Tom Ladds. I'm pretty sure that back in the Squadron days we'd given Tom and his band their first gig. That made me feel pretty old, I must admit! But Tom was a nice chap and easy to get along with. Plus, he was motivated. He hadn't had all the knockbacks we'd experienced and so his attitude was so much more positive. We all needed that and it did rub off on us, at least for a while anyway.

The whole time Tom was in the band, we toured. All this London nonsense wasn't what we were about. When we formed the band it was so we could go out and play places – not so we could sit around in London having the odd show here and there and a photo shoot in Covent Garden to fill the time. Kody was all about playing to the masses, getting drunk and sleeping rough. We went back to basics and it really worked. Kody had a new beginning and the smiles were back.

My mate, Paul Newnham, was a music manager and had been taking an interest in what we were up to for a while. He'd been in bands that had been screwed over by managers so he knew about our side of the coin as well as the business side. It started off with me just calling him for the odd bit of advice here and there. Paul was a top bloke and was

always happy to help us out. We'd toured the album and we'd toured the songs we did with Simon Hanhart; but with this new life of touring came new experiences to write about. I now had tonnes of new tunes and they were going in a different direction to the stuff we were touring.

Paul booked us into a rehearsal studio in London and we all had a few beers and played the new tunes. Basically, he was only there to have a listen and to give some advice on potential studios and producers – but everyone hit it off. We had an absolute blast, and by the end of the rehearsals we were drunk, Paul was our manager, and he was setting us up with a producer.

I'm aware that it sounds like I'm rushing through this but it's literally how it happened. Everything is almost a blur.

We were booked in to record our new single in London with Dave Allen. Dave was The Cure's producer so I was sold on him straightaway. Plus, he was really sarcastic. That sounds like an insult. It isn't. I appreciate sarcasm, and he was full of it.

About two weeks before we were due to start recording, Tom quit the band. He'd been struggling to make rehearsals and gigs and keep up his studying. He was a few years younger than us and was attending college. I totally respected that. He'd only just joined the band, and this lifestyle really isn't for everyone. The rest of us were numbed to it by then. Sleeping in our clothes with woollen hats, scarves and gloves was commonplace for us. We never thought for one minute that we'd probably freeze to death by the side of a busy motorway.

Our big problem now was getting another bass player in and getting them up to speed on our songs enough to record with a decent producer. Turlough brought in his mate, Paul Ruck. Paul was actually a guitarist but he could play bass pretty well and picked up the tracks straightaway. I think it only took a handful of rehearsals and we were ready to go. We went into the studio in London to do three songs in just a few days. We parked up our bus outside the studio. This was our home.

Dave's method of working was pretty chaotic, but we basically had to go with it. Follow the master and don't ask questions.

There was so much weed being smoked while we were recording, and it was playing havoc with my throat. I'm sure I sounded like Joe Cocker by the end of each day. What the weed brought was more crazy ideas from Dave, and more acceptance of the craziness from us. At one point, Dave set up all the recording gear in the bus and told Taffy to start the engine. He recorded the bus running for about ten minutes and then walked back into the studio. There were lots of frowns and whispers of, "What the fuck?" from us. But, like always, we went with it. He was top dog and we certainly weren't in a position to question his methods.

When the recordings came back, they sounded amazing – the best we'd done; and the engine sound he'd put under one of the tracks was incredible. He was a smart bloke, I'll give him that.

We were on such a high after we'd finished that recording. We honestly thought that this was going to be our break. We'd had a couple of "nearly made it" moments in the past but we really thought we'd nailed it with this recording.

We made a couple of music videos with a film company in Guildford. The director's name was Geoff, but for some reason I kept calling him Glenn. I think it might have been the fact that I met him at 9 am after an all-night bender. I was drinking a beer and eating a curry. Not quite the breakfast of champions. But the videos looked great and got a lot of hits and feedback on *YouTube*.

We had a few weeks off from touring and headed home to the Island, where we'd have plenty of time to recharge our batteries. As I said before, the last couple of months had been a blur. Things were happening so fast. It was completely mental.

Life is a weird thing. Sometimes the worst thing you can do is take a break from something. It allows you to reflect and actually look at your life from a different angle. While we were touring, or recording, or doing photo shoots or radio shows, etc., we were distracted from what was really going on. That couple of weeks back on the Isle of Wight brought the last few years down on us like a tonne of bricks.

I can only speak for myself, of course, but I was depressed. I was an alcoholic, and I hadn't even realised it. I had become dependent on drink. I had become dependent on the band and the crowds and the sheer escapism that it all brought.

After a couple of sleepless nights, I actually ended up going to Turlough's to sleep there so I wouldn't be alone. This was an incredibly dark time and there was only one way to put an end to the madness – end Kody itself.

We met in the Solent Inn, where it all began, and after a brief 10-minute chat the band was over. All those years of hard work had burned us out and none of us had anything left to give.

I personally had a huge demon that needed defeating. Something I knew I had to do alone.

We honoured our final show – a half-empty bar in Bembridge on the Isle of Wight. This was where it all ended. It makes me so sad even telling you this. It was so long ago now but it brings all the emotions back. It was a family, and we were walking away from our siblings. I loved every one of them and felt more love than any marriage could ever bring.

The local paper ran with the headline: "Kody Split as Fun Ends". If only they had known the truth. But then people don't want to read about that. People want simple, unemotional endings – truth or not.

So there you have it. A brief background to the stories I'm about to relay. Years of madness condensed into ten thousand words; but hopefully it will help you to understand the tales a bit better.

Now I'm going to get myself another Guinness and then I'll get cracking on my first example of how *NOT* to be a rock star.

You want a beer?

1: THE DRUNKEN MISTAKES OF AMERICA

Midwest, USA, 2002

Band members:
Gareth Icke - Vocals/Guitar
Steve Richmond - Bass
Simon Cook - Drums

You know, sometimes in life you have to take the attitude of: "Fuck it! Sod the consequences, let's just do it and worry about the details later." Some people take that attitude when they get married, or even when they have children, and, while I don't advise it in those particular scenarios, sometimes the "fuck it" attitude is a very positive one.

The band had been going for a little while and, although we'd done sod all in terms of UK tours, we already felt that we'd outgrown England. The fatal mistake we'd made was to believe that the attitudes we encountered on the Isle of Wight were the attitudes of England as a whole. They weren't, and we'd later realise that England was a great place to tour and that only our small town had that small-town mentality.

We felt like we were trying to do something different by playing all original songs when everyone else was still playing covers. But apparently that wasn't cool and we took a fair amount of stick for it from various people. The truth of it was, we were young; and we were learning. Sure, our songs probably sounded somewhat Americanised, but that was what we'd grown up listening to. It would be impossible to expect a bunch of youngsters that grew up listening to the likes of Nirvana and Pearl Jam *not* to have an American twang to their songs. In the end, we lost that and found our own sound; but in the early days, I am sure we did sound like a poor man's Seattle band.

With the invention of the Internet came the ability to have our songs listened to all over the globe. And because of our unintentional American sound, we gathered a fair few followers over there. All we had was home-made recordings, but the Yanks tended to prefer that rawer sound. You wouldn't believe that now when you hear some of the auto-tuned garbage they turn out. But in 2000 and 2001, it was very much still the era of the rock band.

So here we were on the Isle of Wight with a few loyal followers (but also a lot of haters), and on the other side of the world there were groups of people genuinely getting into what we were doing. So Steve, Simon and I decided to "fuck it" and go and play in

America. We'd get the Americans to book us a few shows and we'd worry about flights and accommodation later. If it was meant to be, it was meant to be. And even if things *did* go wrong, all the more rock 'n' roll that was for us. Unless of course we were shot in the face but we never really envisaged that.

So that was that. We had a couple of shows booked up in Madison and Milwaukee in Wisconsin. We decided that the easiest way was to fly to Chicago a week before, try to blag some shows there, and then head up to Wisconsin via bus or train or however way we could. Apart from the flights, nothing was booked; and we'd booked the flights two weeks apart. Two weeks in America and only two shows booked. We'd seriously have to work hard when we got there; but that was fine. Like I said, sometimes in life you just had to say "fuck it". Plus, in terms of the Isle of Wight, in our minds we'd made a massive statement of intent. We weren't just some poor man's Seattle wannabe band; we were a serious band doing serious things. Getting off the Island was a mission too daunting for most bands back then, yet here we were, not just leaving the Island, but leaving the country.

Back then Steve used to work for his family business. It was a wholesale flower- company, which meant he had to drive stupid amounts of miles picking up flowers and dropping them off at various florists across the Isle of Wight. It also meant he had to drive to London twice a week to pick up massive orders coming in from Holland. It seems that nearly every flower in the world has to go through Holland before it's sold. I don't know why I'm telling you that but it's a bit of useless knowledge for you. You never know, it might come up in a pub quiz one day. The point I'm making is that many miles means lots of petrol. And at that time, lots of petrol meant lots of air miles. I think it was BP that was running the promotion; but whoever it was, Steve had air miles coming out of his arse.

We booked three return flights to Chicago, chucked all the air miles in and then whatever money that needed paying on top was thrown in between the three of us. This was also just after 9/11 so the cost of flights had fallen through the floorboards. I think it worked out about £250 each to fly with British Airways all the way to Chicago and back. A bargain considering it costs about £70 to get the three of us and a van the four miles off the Isle of Wight. Man, we get ripped off there! If you ever visit, swim it – with your clothes in a waterproof bag. Much cheaper that way.

I don't think anyone on the Isle of Wight actually thought we were going to do it. The local newspaper ran a piece on it and I think a lot of folks assumed we were just blagging it for the column inches. Well, once the flights were booked, and the shows – albeit only two of them – were posted on our website, people started to realise we were serious. And the thing was, the three of us got along really well anyway, so even if it ended up being just a couple of shows, we'd have a cracking time on the beer in America – a lads' holiday if nothing else.

We flew from London, and it wasn't two minutes into the flight when we were already scamming British Airways for whatever we could get. Free *beer?* Were they *kidding?* None of us had ever flown anything but budget airlines before and so the prospect of free beer was too much to handle. Back then, although we were young, we were already hardened drinkers. We knew that this free-beer lark wouldn't continue for the entire flight unless we worked out some sort of plan.

I would get up and ask one stewardess for three beers. Once I'd got them, we'd then hide them under our seats. Steve would then collar another stewardess and do the same, and then so would Simon. We then had three beers each and that would keep us going for a while. As soon as we ran out, I would go and ask a different stewardess for three beers and so the cycle continued. There were three stewardesses in our entire cabin, and the way we worked it out we'd have at least nine cans of beer before any of us would have to go back to the same stewardess. And that would be fine, as in her mind we'd only had three. So the cycle could start all over again. You can consume a lot of beer in eight hours.

After a while though, the beer dried up. Then the wine dried up. And, after a brief three- way conversation between the stewardesses, our plan was foiled. We'd drunk them dry though. That was rock 'n' roll if nothing else. We were from the Isle of Wight! We didn't know about common courtesy and stuff like that!

When we landed in the US, the three of us were pretty battered. That didn't go down well. I've never seen a more paranoid country in my life. I'm sure they think everyone is a suicide bomber. Getting through Customs was an absolute nightmare. We were hauled into different rooms, made to fill out a million different forms and asked a billion stupid questions. They wanted to know everything about our trip and everything about us as people. I thought they were going to ask to see a picture of my girlfriend's breasts; it was getting that in depth.

One thing I should also tell you about Steve is that if there was a simple way of doing something, he'd do the polar opposite. I'd put my guitar in a guitar case and my clothes in a bag. Simon had his snare drum and cymbals in a case and his clothes in a bag. But Steve was trying to save money on extra luggage. So he'd put all his clothes in a suitcase, then unbolted the neck of his bass guitar and placed the two parts in his suitcase and wrapped them in clothes. Now that sounds like a reasonable idea.

Simon and I would have to pay an extra couple of quid for our musical instruments, whereas Steve wouldn't. What Steve had failed to realise was that post-9/11, security at American airports had stepped up massively. And when a suitcase full of metal, wood and wire went through the scanner, it was going to create some suspicion amongst the staff. It bloody did, and it took what felt like an eternity to get through security.

All of our instruments were taken out and tossed around. I'm not trying to be smutty by using the word "instruments" as a euphemism, by the way. We weren't strip-searched,

but our guitars were manhandled and probably felt quite cheap and used after they'd been finished with. The security guards were swabbing down everything and testing the samples for explosives. They had giant dogs sniffing their way through our clothes. It was all very odd and pretty intimidating, to be honest. But in the end, they found nothing and so let us through the gates and into the big wide world that is the United States of America.

We hailed a cab and headed into the city. None of us had ever been to Chicago before so we didn't really have much of a clue what to expect. We had a week to settle before we had a show anyway, so as far as we were concerned, we'd chill for a couple of days, sleep out our jet lag and we'd take on the city when we were less fragile.

We'd booked a motel online for the first few nights, and then once we found our feet we'd either stay there or move on to someplace else. Well, the beauty of booking online was that we could set things up in advance so there was no panic when we landed. The bad side of booking online is that you know nothing about the area, and the images on the website are often very different from the reality you encounter upon arrival.

"Where you heading, bro?" asked the cabbie. Wow! They actually talk like that? I thought it was just how they spoke in sitcoms. But nope, we were "bros" apparently.

Steve got the motel reservation ticket from out of his bag. "Umm... a place called Berwyn, mate." The cabbie swung round. "You shittin' me?" "Nope."

That's not the reaction you're looking for from a cab driver who's about to drive you to your accommodation. None of us wanted to ask why he'd reacted like that, and so none of us did. We just shut up and tried to take in the scenery. We'd been driving for about 10 minutes and I said to the guys, "This area looks pretty plush!" Then we drove another 10 minutes and that became, "This is all right, isn't it?" We were driving for about 45 minutes in the end, and with every 10 minutes the area gradually got more and more scary.

"Here y'all are, boys." On the Isle of Wight, I was a man. But here in Berwyn, I was nothing but a very lost, very confused boy.

I don't know if you know Chicago at all, but basically the area we were staying was the equivalent of the Bronx in New York. I have no idea what the area's like now, but back then we stuck out like dislocated thumbs. We were three skinny white guys, with small-town English accents in one of the toughest areas of one of the USA's major cities. This was going to take some working out.

It was dark when we arrived so we chucked our bags in the room, grabbed some beers from over the road and barricaded ourselves in the room. We were all pretty shattered from the journey and there was no way we were going to test the area in the dark. Our American adventure would start in the morning, but until then we'd lie in bed drinking beer and watching the New York Rangers take on the New York Islanders at ice hockey. American tour or not, that was the perfect night for me. I played ice hockey back then and I adored the New York Rangers. And there's nothing like a local derby to get the juices flowing. Simon fell asleep; and I'm not surprised – it was a crap game. Steve stayed awake, more as moral support for me, and I think because we had lived together he had secretly become a bit of a Rangers' fan himself.

I'll never forget it. It was 0–0 and heading into overtime when Brian Leetch smashed one from the edge of the zone and straight into the bottom corner. 1–0 to the Rangers. Get in! Steve and I leapt off the bed, waking up Simon. The game finished just a few seconds later and that was that. What a result!

This trip was destined to be a success, I thought. Okay, the area was ropey but I was sure we'd settle in. We had beer and a motel room and, despite the odd bit of shouting from one of the other rooms, it wasn't too bad. Plus, the Rangers had just beaten the Islanders. That's like Derby County beating Nottingham Forest. Then, just as we'd allowed ourselves to start thinking positively again after being dropped into a potential gun-crime hotbed, they interrupted the post-match interviews for a news conference from the White House.

"This can't be good."

And sure enough, it wasn't good. The USA and Britain had just declared war on Iraq. Brilliant. They had to bloody wait until we'd arrived before becoming embroiled in yet another conflict overseas! We didn't really know how that would affect us while we were in the USA. Maybe it wouldn't at all, but then again maybe it would. Maybe there would be uprisings in the less wealthy suburbs (that's what tends to happen when your government goes ahead and fulfils its agenda without consulting its people. There is no money for healthcare but plenty of money for bombs).

We were smack bang in the centre of one of the poorer areas. I mean, it was March, and it was pretty cold, but I didn't fancy warming my palms on a burned-out police car. And as far as we were concerned, that was a distinct possibility.

I'm sure I'm making us sound like pussies, but the truth was we felt out of our depth. In the first couple of days we would get the "L" train into the centre of Chicago and hang out. Then, someone threatened to blow up Sears Tower and even the city centre didn't seem like a safe place to be. But, we didn't let it deter us, and we gradually relaxed and began to feel safe. We'd hang out in music shops and get chatting to musicians about the best places to get a gig and stuff. Plus, we'd have great fun winding up the locals in coffee shops. One of our particular favourites was to be sat down at a table, and then to call over a local for a chat. It was pretty easy to strike up a conversation as our English accent was appealing, for some reason.

Steve would be sat next to me but would lie across my lap so he was out of sight. I'd then say, "Excuse me?" and strike up a conversation with someone who had just walked into the coffee shop. After a couple of minutes of chat about local venues and the best place to get a show, Steve would then rise from my lap, wiping his mouth. I'd pretend to do up my flies while carrying on the conversation like nothing had happened. People didn't find that as amusing as I'd hoped. Apparently, Americans don't have a sense of humour after all.

We also found that out in a Foot Locker sports store. I saw a baseball cap with "ROCK HARD" embroidered on it and then Simon found one with "COCKS" plastered across it. Well it's obvious what you do, isn't it? You put them next to each other and you take a photo? That got us physically removed from the store. I think they were secretly just disappointed that they hadn't thought of it first.

So, that was how we spent the first couple of days in Chicago – messing about and having a laugh. But as soon as night fell, we would stock up on booze and lock ourselves in the motel room. We'd worked out a route from our motel to the train station, and that was the only part of Berwyn that we'd allow ourselves to see. It was such an intimidating area and none of us would feel comfortable being out after dark.

We grabbed a few local magazines and started making some calls. Eventually, we had our first show booked. It was a couple of days later in an area just outside the city. It meant getting a train and all that nonsense, but we didn't care. We had a show in America. That was something to tell the folks back home. We'd done it.

The next morning, we all decided that we weren't going to be confined to our motel for another two days. We'd come all this way, and since we didn't have a show for a couple of days we may as well treat it like a holiday and enjoy ourselves. It was March, so it was pretty cold there. We all had big parka-style jackets which made us look bigger than we were. Plus, Simon was a billion feet tall, and

Steve and I were both well over six foot. Our plan was simple – walk around like we owned the place. People smell fear in the same way that a dog does; so instead of exuding fear, we'd exude confidence. Yeah, we were English but we were also pretty big blokes and none of the people around Berwyn knew who the fuck we were. Maybe we were people not to be messed with. Maybe we were some new English-based mafia group that had come to plant a flag of dominance in Chicago. I know that's a bit over-the-top but we thought we'd go with that attitude nonetheless.

We strolled around the local area like we had every right to call it our own. We were polite to people but we puffed out our chests and made it clear that we weren't intimidated by them. All of us were secretly bricking it but we put on enough front to keep the fear hidden.

We walked for ages, and eventually we came to an area of disused buildings and what looked like closed-down factories. Not the most sensible place to be walking. The first thing that tourists are told by travel reps is to keep to the busy and well-lit areas, and avoid walking into the most secluded or run-down parts of town. All of a sudden, we turned a corner to be faced with a large group of what looked like homeless people. Not the type of homeless people that lay on the streets of London with a dog, but the type of homeless people that kidnap you and then turn you into a stew.

All in one movement, we turned the corner and then continued to turn until we were facing back in the direction we'd come from.

"Keep walking, lads."

But it was too late; we'd been spotted. One in the group was a woman. Well, at least she sounded like a woman. It was kind of hard to tell.

"Hey, Sticks! I'm the sticks around here!"

Sticks? Who the fuck was sticks? We all turned around and they were walking towards us. I felt like Michael Jackson's date in the Thriller video.

She continued. "Get your sticks out, boy."

Being the naïve Englishman that I am, I assumed that "sticks" was some street slang for money. So I grabbed a couple of bucks and handed it to her. She said thanks, but was still more concerned about the "sticks". It turns out that Simon, for some reason, had drumsticks in his back pocket, and when we'd turned around to scarper she'd spotted them.

Five minutes later, Simon had one stick, the homeless woman had the other, and the two of them were playing some Jamaican-style drum beat on a metal oil drum. Not wanting to offend, Steve and I were dancing around in the street with several bearded homeless blokes. If you'd asked me to describe what was about to happen when we turned that corner, it certainly wouldn't have been an impromptu street carnival.

We danced for a bit, and gave them some more money for god knows what. Smack, probably. And then we were on our way back to what passed for civilisation.

There was a bar around the corner from our motel that we'd been far too intimidated to go into. Well, that night we weren't. That night we were three double-hard bastards and if we wanted a drink, damn straight we were going to get a drink. The three of us walked in and instantly the place fell silent and people looked at us. It wasn't a very big bar; in fact, it was probably about the size of someone's front room. But that meant we couldn't skulk off and find a corner to hide in. We took up three stools at the bar.

"Two Jim Beams and a Jack Daniels please, barman."

The guy just stared at us. He looked just like one of those murderous bikers from a Hells Angels film. He had long grey hair and his tattoo-covered body was on show, apart from a black leather waistcoat.

"Sure," he said, in a gruff Clint-Eastwood-style voice. "These are on me."

I wasn't expecting that. And although I should have been grateful that the guy was giving us free drinks, I couldn't help but think it was like a killer giving his victim an expensive cigar before shooting him. That's what happens in the films at least. And America is basically one big movie set.

"Thanks."

"No worries. You're British?"

"English, yeah."

None of us ever considered ourselves British. We're English. I think the Scots and Welsh would also agree; there is a distinct difference.

The barman walked out to the back and was gone for a couple of minutes. I was thinking that this was the part where he came out with a sawn-off shotgun and informed us that they didn't welcome posh talking, tea drinking Brits here. Instead, he came out with a television and placed it on the bar in front of us. The drinks were one thing but

I'd never seen a barman give away a TV before. He plugged it in and was faffing about with the aerial. The bloke could see we were looking quite confused as to what was going on.

"You're English, right? You love soccer? David Beckham?"

We all said, "Yeah, of course," even though Simon actually hated football.

The guy pressed a couple of buttons and up popped ESPN. It was Aston Villa versus Manchester United. What a result! And to think we'd felt intimidated to go in there. We'd only been in the pub five minutes and already we had free whiskys and the barman had set up our very own football TV at the bar. We would be locals in there from now on!

When we finally got to play our gig, it was the biggest travelling hassle I've ever experienced. The venue was just a "few" stops out of Chicago, but what we failed to realise was that in America, the distances are a fair bit bigger. It turned out that it was about 10 stops from Berwyn into the city centre, and then about fifty miles on a massive double-decker train out to the where the venue was. We were led to believe the venue was in the suburbs of Chicago. It was probably nearer to the suburbs of Los Angeles in all truth.

When we arrived, we asked a fellah where the venue was and he said, "Just a couple of blocks that way." Now you'd think we'd have learned that USA distances are slightly
bigger than average, and booked a cab. But no, we decided to walk. The "block" went on forever and the three of us were struggling with our gear. Then just as we got to the crest of a hill, the sidewalk disappeared. I was expecting to see the shining lights of a music venue, not the shining lights of oncoming trucks. We just kept walking for what felt like a lifetime until we reached the freeway.

"Was that bastard winding us up?!"

Just as we were about to give up and stroll back to the station to hunt down the man with the dodgy directions, Steve spotted a sign pointing to a live-music venue. So, on we plodded across various lanes of speeding traffic until we finally reached the place. To be fair, it was worth the walk as the venue was awesome. It had a massive stage with some seriously expensive gear, and a really cool bar area. The bar looked like something you'd find on a beach in Brazil, not off the freeway in Illinois. There was an offer on bottles of Corona, and because of our accent we were immediately adored. Now, this I could get used to.

We played the show with a couple of local bands and it went really well. Obviously, we were a fair bit nervous and it wasn't ideal using other people's amps and stuff, but we drank through it. We hadn't travelled all this way to perform nervously and not enjoy it. We were gigging in the USA and damn straight we were going to have it!

Steve and I had this moody stage persona in those days. Off stage we'd get pissed up and crack jokes but when we were on stage we went for that "moody and mysterious" look. I reckon we both thought women liked it, but the truth was we'd only ever really attract weird self-harmers. All the regular laid-back girls probably thought we'd be hard work and atmosphere-dampening. You live and you learn and all that. That night though, no matter how moody and deep that we wanted to appear, it wasn't going to happen because we both kept laughing.

One of the lads at the venue was obsessed with recording all the bands that played there – which was great because it meant we got a copy of our set on CD. It also meant the stage was set up differently. The guy was so concerned that the sound of the drums would spill out into the other microphones that he boxed Simon in behind this Plexiglas wall. I know it doesn't sound that funny now, but at the time it really tickled me and Steve. We were quite an energetic band that relied a fair bit on crowd interaction, and there was our drummer locked up behind some Plexiglas prison wall. Simon wasn't impressed because he couldn't hear my guitar that well, but as far as Steve and I were concerned, the more pissed off Simon looked in his cage, the more it amused us. There were a few occasions when I did well to hold back the giggles long enough to spit out the words to the songs. You know when you shouldn't laugh, and that's when you laugh the most? I'm a sucker for that.

So, our opening US performance had gone well. We were given a lift back to the station by one of the other bands and hopped onto the last train back into Chicago. The journey back was going to be a race against time as we would have to connect with the last train to Berwyn, and if we missed that it would mean a very expensive cab ride. We were all totally over-the-moon with how our first show had gone. We'd actually done it. We'd got off our small-town arses and travelled thousands of miles across the globe to perform. And not only that, but we'd been well received. That was a major coup for all three of us.

We pulled into Union Station and started running. We had to get out of the station and a couple of blocks across to where our "L" train would take us back to Berwyn. When we stepped outside of the station, it was sheer carnage.

"What the fuck happened?"

"Steve, did you leave a cigarette burning?"

Downtown Chicago was trashed. There were police absolutely everywhere. People were running in all directions, but mainly from the direction we were meant to be heading in. We just stood there for a few seconds trying to take it all in. There were thousands of people everywhere – some bleeding and some shouting abuse at the scores of police that were now covering almost every angle. A young lad came running past and then hid in a shop doorway just up from where we were stood.

"Mate, what the fuck's going on?!" We asked him.

It was a massive anti-war protest that, due to heavy-handed police, had turned into chaos (it's often the way – throw a few uniforms and batons into the middle of a peaceful protest and it tends not to remain peaceful for very long).

He went on to explain that there were over 50,000 protesters, and that there was more than four times that number in New York at the same time. That's a serious number of people in a country that is still pretty clueless when it comes to what's really going on across the planet. They tend to swallow whatever bullshit they're fed on CNN and carry on regardless. But with this many people protesting it was bound to cause shockwaves across the nation. Or so you'd think.

Steve, Simon and I still had a train to catch, and although we wanted to stick around and take in what was left of the atmosphere, we didn't really want to do it while carrying expensive musical equipment.

We just about made the last train and piled back to our motel in Berwyn. All three of us couldn't wait to get back to put the news on. That must have been an incredible sight. I mean, we'd only come back to see the very last part of the demonstration, but with 50,000 people it must have been mental. We watched CNN, we watched Fox News, ABC, you name it – and there was nothing. There had been 200,000 people in New York and 50,000 people in Chicago. And that was all *we* knew about. What about all the other major cities across the USA? How many people had protested in LA, Miami, Philadelphia? But instead CNN ran a massive piece on three fat women in Alabama

whose sons were fighting in Iraq. They were obviously pro-war and were speaking of how proud they were that their sons were fighting for democracy. Pull the other one. I've always know the media was corrupt but I think this was the first time that Steve and Simon had seen it in action.

"That's fucking unbelievable!"

But it wasn't unbelievable. It was the media for you – reporting only what the government wants its people to hear.

"Welcome to the land of the free, boys."

We had a show booked in Madison and a show booked in Milwaukee. The Madison show wasn't for a couple of days but we figured we'd pile up there earlier. We'd seen Chicago and, to be honest, we'd kind of had enough of the place. It was okay, but like all major cities it didn't really welcome people with open arms. Everyone is so busy getting on with their own lives that others become invisible. London is very much like that and I would imagine pretty much every major city across the globe has the same traits. Madison was a smaller place and so we figured, with our little US knowledge, that it would also be friendlier. When I say smaller, I'm talking on an American scale. It was still a pretty massive place.

We looked at all the different ways of travelling and there was only one that we could even nearly afford. That was the Greyhound bus. I hate coaches as they always make me feel sick, but we couldn't afford the train, and in rock 'n' roll circles, the Greyhound was kind of cool. There isn't a decent American film that doesn't mention it at some point. So we bought our tickets and prepared for the three-hour journey to Madison.

This journey taught me two things: The first is, when travelling as a threesome you must board the coach in the first two or you end up sat next to a weird Chinese woman. And the second is, when a fight between a group of heavy-set black guys kicks off at the back of the coach, don't swing around and say loudly, "What the fuck is going on back there?" These are life lessons I have taken with me.

To be fair, the only reaction my "What the fuck is going on back there?" got me was a very stern, "What?!" But that was enough to make me shit myself. It's the films, you see – they make you think that everyone in America is going to blow your head off with a semi-automatic weapon.

The journey wasn't comfortable, as the buses are designed to get as many poor people crammed in as possible. That was fine for the Oriental woman next to me – her legs hardly reached the floor. Steve, Simon and I, on the other hand, would forever be disabled as a result of that journey.

What kept us going was the scenery. America really is vast, and it's not until you get out on the open road that you realise just how vast it is. Plus, there would be a toilet break

and leg-stretch at Green Bay. I can't stand American Football, but when I saw the Green Bay Packers' stadium I was like a kid at Christmas.

"Steve, Simon, there's the Green Bay Packers' stadium!"

"So? Didn't think you liked American Football?"

"I don't. But I do like urinating and having blood flow through my legs."

I've been in some public toilets before. I'm not proud of it but I've seen some pretty gross sights. Piss- and shit-covered floors are pretty commonplace around the world. I've even seen the odd pile of vomit here and there. In fact, once I was stood having a piss when someone threw a turd out of the cubicle and it hit someone on the shoulder. However, I had not yet experienced what I saw at Green Bay Greyhound station.

As we walked into the toilets, they were packed; so I went to have a wee in one of the cubicles. As I reached down to lift the seat, I was greeted with a quite incredible sight. Someone had been kind enough to leave a rather large pile of semen sat on top of the toilet seat. Who has a wank on a toilet seat?! Only in America.

We arrived in Madison and booked into a Red Roof Inn. They're pretty much the same set-up as Travelodge in the UK – cheap and no-frills but they are clean and they do the trick. Ours was a short bus ride out of town but was directly opposite a giant mall. It had bars and restaurants and a bowling alley and stuff – plenty of things to keep us amused. I think the room worked out at about $70 a night. That was about £40 and, shared between three of us, we were happy with that. We were set up in Madison. All we needed now was some gigs.

That evening we grabbed the local paper and headed, on foot, across an eight-lane freeway to an Applebee's in the mall. Applebee's was a sort of steak house, but it wasn't expensive and we felt we'd treat ourselves to some fat American food.

We had a few beers, shitloads of grub, and, in the local paper, we found a couple of open mic nights in the area. We figured that would be a good way to meet local musicians and blag ourselves a few gigs here and there. While finding the open mic nights was great, I was more concerned with the waitress. I'd never seen a more beautiful woman in my life. And it wasn't just the beer goggles either. I was besotted. Problem was, she knew it and she ended up overcharging me ten dollars because she knew I wouldn't complain. I didn't. I felt she'd earned it by looking so stunning. How shallow does that make me sound? I was young.

The following night we got a cab into the city and played at an open mic night. The guy was really cool, and because we were from so far away he gave us a longer time-slot. So it was pretty much a gig of our own. He also booked us two gigs at his mate's bar for the next two evenings. What a result! If things are meant to be, they are meant to be. And sometimes in life, you just need to allow yourself these positive things by putting

yourself in the position to receive them. I know I sound like a hippie, but I believe that's true.

Another band on that night was a group called The Shivers. They were American but were obsessed with British bands and British culture. They were instantly our new best friends and we spent the night getting royally battered on the local beers. This was the life! Performing in the USA, getting drunk and talking punk rock. As a 21-year-old, this was my nirvana.

There are two types of taxi cab in Madison. There is the regular cab, which is pretty pricey; and then there is the Badger Cab, which is cheap. It's a no-brainer – you take the cheapest option every time. We had no idea why they were cheaper but that didn't really matter to us. As long as we got from A to B, we were cool. So we booked up a Badger Cab from the venue back to our hotel. As it turns out, the reason Badger Cabs are cheap is because they're "sharing" cabs. If someone phones up in a similar area, the driver will pick them up too and thus save money on petrol. That didn't really bother us as the three of us were in the back, so whoever they had to pick up would have to go in the front anyway.

We piled in the taxi and it starting heading towards the freeway. Then they get a call for another pick up. We drove for what felt like an hour all over the city to pick this person up. Surely there was a car nearer to them than we were? Apparently not. So we finally reach the guy in what can only be described as Berwyn, Chicago, Mark II.

What was it with us and these areas? We were drawn to them like moths to a flamethrower. The lad got in the cab and then it all kicked off in the front. Turns out that this chap is a bit of a fare dodger and our taxi driver won't pick him up. Only problem with that being that the fellah is already in the passenger seat with his seatbelt on. So this argument is going on and on. The guy won't get out of the car and the driver won't drive. So here we are in a stalemate situation. The three of us were battered and just wanted to sleep, but instead we were sat in the projects watching an argument. After a while, the passenger got the message and got out. What a waste of time and effort that was! I'd rather have paid the extra money and got a normal taxi. We'd avoid Badger Cabs in future.

The following morning we were woken by a loud banging on the motel-room window.

"Go away!" was the joint cry. We were all hungover to hell and we all needed to sleep. We just assumed it was the cleaner coming to change the bedsheets and stuff. I was sharing a double bed with Steve; it was pretty seedy whether the sheets were clean or not.

"Guys! Wake up!"

The three of us looked at each other. Who the hell could that be? I opened the curtains dressed only in boxer shorts, and stood there was Matt, the singer of the Shivers, and his girlfriend.

"You guys are staying with us. No point wasting your money on motels."

How amazing was that?! So we packed our bags, loaded up Matt's car and drove into the city. Apart from Matt's exhaust pipe, we all arrived safely at their house. The exhaust pipe was left somewhere on the freeway a couple of miles back.

We spent the day in pubs around Madison before heading to the venue for the show. The bar was really cool and did the best pizzas you could imagine. It looked just like a regular Italian restaurant from the outside; but as you walked in, stairs took you down to the basement. It was awesome. There were a few tables and chairs and a pool table, but mainly people just stood around the bar.

The deal was free pizzas and free beer in exchange for playing our set. That seemed like a pretty cool deal to me. After all, we didn't have to pay for a hotel room now and we could certainly drink a fair bit. It would probably work out that we were getting paid more by doing the deal than we would if we were to be paid in cash.

So, we played our set and once again went down a storm. That was three shows and three great receptions. This American tour lark was easy! We sold a few CDs and that helped put a couple of quid back in our pockets. We'd gone to America for the experience and we were certainly having that. See, that's the difference between playing abroad and playing in the UK. People abroad actually applaud the fact that you play original songs. In England people always wanted covers. We never saw the point in that after a while. Sure, I get it when you're starting out; but after a while you have to go original.

The other thing that went in our favour in America was the banter. Not that many bands say much on stage, and if they do it's normally to big themselves up. We were the polar opposite. We just used to take the piss out of ourselves, and people loved that. It broke the ice with the audience and we managed to connect with people. That's the hardest part, I think. In the words of Thom Yorke: anyone can play guitar.

After our set we all walked up to the bar. We were drinking this beer called Brown Cow or something. It was local to Madison and was pretty good. Tasted like Newcastle Brown Ale. You know that stuff? Well yeah, it was like that. There was this woman sat at the bar chatting to the barman. We ordered our beers and when the barman went to pour them, I got chatting to her. She said she'd enjoyed the show and all that generic shit people say when a band's just walked off stage. I was smitten. She was absolutely stunning and my jaw was quite clearly on the floor. It was pointless pursuing because I was a skinny young English bloke and, where she was slightly older – and gorgeous – she'd be looking for a more manly man. Much like the barman in fact. He was a pretty big hairy bloke. A good-looking chap, but big. You know – the American look. He probably chopped down trees during the day before getting into a boozy fight at night.

The barman brought our beers over and sat back down behind the bar. Steve and Simon cleared off to play pool and so I was left there with the girl. I was in an awkward situation because I was in mid conversation with her, and at the same time it was pretty clear that the barman was trying to work his magic. Sod it, I wasn't from round there; I'd just keep chatting to her and see what happened. The two of us had a laugh and were getting along pretty well – much to the distaste of the lumberjack, I might add. In the end, he snapped. Now, obviously he was trying to impress this girl so he couldn't exactly get angry with me; but what he *could* do, or at least try to do, was show me up.

He was a big bloke and I was a scrawny young boy. Surely he could have picked a million different ways to show me up for what I was. An arm wrestle? A game of pool? Either of those would have defeated me. But, no; he chose drinking. That's not particularly smart really, as one thing Americans cannot do is drink.

"Shots? You and me?" he said.

I looked at the girl for approval and she rolled her eyes then smirked. I took that as a "go for it", so I did.

"Sure. You choose the first set," I said.

Then he comes back and pours out two shots of apple Schnapps. Was he being serious? Schnapps?! So I skulled it and then it was my choice. I pointed to the top shelf. There was a bottle of whisky covered in cobwebs.

"Let's do that one."

The guy hesitated and then dragged it down. I think we only did a couple of shots of the stuff and the fellah was already struggling. The lads called me over to play pool, so I thanked the barman for his hospitality, told the beautiful brunette that it was lovely to meet her and then walked away.

"What the fuck did you do to that barman? He can barely stand up," said Steve. "Yanks can't handle their booze, mate."

The next night, we were back at the same place again. Only this time we'd play our set and then it was a free-for-all afterwards. Anyone who wanted to play a song or two was allowed to get up and do their worst. It was packed again but was a slightly harder crowd. I hate playing to other musicians as they always judge and think they can do better. Even if they could, what's the point of making a band feel uncomfortable? I've never understood that. But there you go.

We had a pizza, played our set and, once again, set up stall at the bar. We were on the Brown Cow but I figured it was only a matter of time before I got challenged to go on to something harder. Men can be so competitive when it comes to their "manhood".

The beautiful girl was sat in the same place as the night before, but there was a different barman. I sat down next to her and we started chatting like we'd known each other for 10 years. She was well out of my league. Surely she wasn't flirting with me? She *was*, y'know, and I was lapping it up. Just as I felt like I might be getting somewhere, the new barman sidles over.

"Wanna do some shots?"

"Sure. But not that Schnapps crap."

"Hell, no! We're doing the hard stuff!"

Okay, I liked this barman better than the last one. He looked the complete opposite, too. He was skinny, clean shaven and black. The fellah the night before was big, hairy and white. We did a couple of shots from the cobweb-covered whiskey bottle and then the barman walked off and left us alone to carry on talking. Unlike the barman the night before, this one could handle his drink but wasn't trying to compete – he was just being nice. I was glad because the way he knocked back the drink, I think I'd have been in for a bigger battle than the night before.

The girl stood up and said, "This is me," and then walked towards the stage. Not content with looking like Pocahontas, *she sang as well?* She looked at me and said, "This is for the English boy," and proceeded to play a beautiful song by Jewel. The whole bar was looking at me. I knew what they were thinking. They were wondering how the bloody hell I'd managed to blag that. I know they were thinking that because I was thinking the same.

She finished and came and sat back down next to me. She was incredible. I don't know how I'd managed to make her think I was a real man. I certainly wasn't, that's for sure. Steve and Simon came over and we ordered a shot each of the hardcore whisky. Well, this was where I let my true colours shine out. As the barman poured them, Simon asked what the whisky was called.

"Knob Creek, sir."

"It probably will when I get old, yeah," I said.

Simon and Steve laughed, but the barman and Pocahontas just looked confused. I then made the fatal error of explaining to her that in England a "knob" is another word for a penis, and that's why it was funny. If I'd have left it there, I might have been okay. But no, the three of us then started making penis jokes for the next 10 minutes. She fake- laughed a couple of times and then did that whole oh-my-goodness-is-that-the-time speech. I'd wrecked it, and she left. But then I thought, who doesn't like penis jokes?! They're funny. Simple as that.

We had one more night in Madison before we had to make our way over to Milwaukee for our show there. We were due to do a late-night radio interview, so beer was definitely off the agenda. I'm not sure how many people the show went out to but we thought we should try to be at least a little bit professional about it. Even if 20 people tuned in, they were 20 new potential fans. We should try to come across well.

Simon, Steve and I, and the guys from The Shivers decided to do something distinctly American. It doesn't get a lot more US of A than a few games of bowling. So the load of us piled in to the local bowling alley for a few games before the interview. The place was a shithole and was full of overweight blokes with personalised shirts. I was waiting for Homer Simpson to walk in but he never showed up.

Our lane was the only one that wasn't scoring a strike on every throw. You should really appreciate other people for being very good at something; but when it comes to bowling it's not that cool really, is it? Personalised shirts, gloves, hats, bowling balls – it's all quite tragic really. I needed a beer.

Steve and I went to the bar. We figured that one drink wouldn't hurt. It was almost rude not to have a beer when you went bowling. It's a rite of passage or something, isn't it?

"Two pints of Bud, please, mate?"

"You can get a four-pint pitcher of Bud for $5."

Steve and I looked at each other.

"Two pitchers of Bud, please, mate."

That was the beginning of the end. You can't sell beer that cheap and not expect us to abuse it. They were to blame really, weren't they? By the time Matt drove us to the radio station, the three of us were pretty hammered. Luckily we were pretty good at hiding it, and because it was so late even the sober folks looked pretty bleary-eyed.

As soon as we walked into the station, we were taken into a separate room and briefed on what we could and couldn't say. No swearing, no racism, no mentioning the war in Iraq ... There were a million rules and there was no way we were going to remember them all. So we thought we'd just rely on our common sense and we'd be fine. It would have been okay had it not been for the Budweiser promotion.

The interview started off great and the DJ was really cool and created a chilled-out environment. It basically felt like we were chatting with our mates over a few beers. Then he spotted I was wearing a "Something Corporate" T-shirt. They were an American band that we were really into at the time.

"So you're a 'Something Corporate' fan then, hey?"

"Yeah, saw them live last week actually."

"Oh, really? They good live?"

"They're fucking amazing!"

The studio went silent. Well, almost silent. I panicked and said, "Oh, shit! I swore." Yeah, nice one, Gareth. Way to get yourself out of a hole. Swearing again will help.

Steve and Simon were in hysterics. The DJ swiftly flicked on a track and we all hoped no- one had picked up on the swearing. Of course they had; I mean it was as clear as day. But that was my one fuck-up. We were new to this interview lark so we had to be allowed one mistake. We put it down to nerves and moved on.

The rest of the interview went well and we thought we'd got away with it. That was until the frictions between England, Scotland and Wales were brought up. The interviewer had spent some time in the UK and started talking about the fact that it isn't the United Kingdom at all. The individual nations are actually fans of each other.

"Nah, Scotland hates England, England hates Scotland, Wales hates England, and so on."

"Being an Englishman, who do you blame for that?"

"The Irish."

Again, silence. See, I thought I was being funny, but apparently not. Apparently that constituted racism and so I'd managed to break the first two rules of our little pre- interview chat. The Americans can be so uptight. Oh well, at least we knew we wouldn't be invited back on *that* station again.

That night, or, should I say, that morning, we all piled back to The Shivers' house. It was your typical middle-American pad. You know the kind. We've seen it in the films – the giant wooden house with the big terraced front. It looked like the kind of place where you'd expect to see Clint Eastwood sitting outside in a rocking chair, cradling a shotgun. In fact, it looked like the kind of area where cradling a shotgun was commonplace.

The place was enormous, with a converted cellar that they used as a rehearsal space. To say I was envious was an understatement. Their house was quality, and they were awesome for letting us stay.

The next morning, I woke up with a cat doing what dogs do to strangers' legs, to me. I'm not sure why I felt the need to tell you that. But now at least part of it is out of my head and into yours. Enjoy that mental image, why don't you. I didn't even know cats did that humping thing?

Because we were English, Matt and his Mrs thought that we must be obsessed with drinking tea. To be honest, I think the obsession was more their own as their cupboards were full of the stuff. None of us were that bothered about tea but we were polite and necked a load of it out of courtesy. We figured it was pretty cool that they were trying to make us feel at home.

It was our last show that night and we were playing just down the road in Milwaukee. When I say "down the road" I mean in US-terms. It was probably a hundred miles or so away. This show was the main gig of the tour and had been booked by a local girl called Maria. I'd had a few online conversations with her, but apart from that we didn't really know her at all. And we didn't know much about the show. But that fitted in to our "fuck it" category. We'd applied that mindset to the entire tour and it had looked after us. We crossed our fingers and hoped for more of the same.

I had a quick chat with Maria on the phone and in no time she was outside.

"Is that her?"

"I don't fucking know."

I walked outside and towards a white car.

"Maria?"

"Sure is."

We were in. She couldn't have been driving a more American car. It was proper old- school with a bench seat in the front. I wish I knew more about cars so I could describe it in more detail. It was old and white with red leather seats. I almost expected to find the remains of JFK's skull on the back seat. It was that style of motor.

Steve, Simon and I grabbed all of our stuff out of the all-American house and stuffed it into the all-American vehicle. We really were lapping up the culture. We just needed some cowboy boots and a gun rack and we would have been fully Americanised.

We said goodbye to Matt and the guys from The Shivers, but not before they'd managed to stuff a bag full of "English Breakfast" tea bags into my suitcase. Their hospitality knew no bounds, apparently. We hugged, high-fived and were on our way out of Madison.

You're probably wondering why I keep mentioning the tea, aren't you? There is a good reason, I promise. Well, it's not a good reason. Not good for me anyway. I'll explain later.

Maria drove us up to Milwaukee and found us a Red Roof Inn near the airport. We really should have called the tour The Red Roof Tour. At least then we could have asked for some sponsorship.

So we chucked our stuff into the room and made our way to the venue. We were playing a place called Vnuk's. It was a much bigger place than any of the venues we'd played on the tour so far. And looking at the set-up and the gear, this wasn't a muck-about establishment – this was the real deal.

Kody was on second out of three. That's the most perfect slot as you're guaranteed a large audience. The other two bands were both from Milwaukee and had a decent following. We'd just sit nicely in the middle and play to their fans. When we played

shows at home, we always fished for that slot. If you open, it's normally quiet; and if you headline as an out-of-town band, a lot of the people leave after their mates' bands and you play to a quiet venue. This way we would be sorted with a crowd.

We did our soundcheck and the sound was huge. It was just the three of us but if you closed your eyes you'd think it was a full eight-piece rock band. It was the first time we'd ever experienced a sound as massive and professional as that. It seems you can polish a turd after all!

We had a fair bit of time to kill before we went on stage so we all grabbed a stool and propped ourselves up at the bar.

"Newcastle Brown on tap?!"

It's the little things that get you the most excited, I guess. The barman just laughed and came over with three plastic pint-cups.

"Here you go, lads. Free refills for the band members."

Vnuk's was to be renamed "Heaven on Earth" from now on. It had an amazing sound, an ever-growing audience, Kody posters all over the place and free Newcastle Brown Ale on tap. Throw in a couple of cherubs and a bearded guy and you've got yourself through the Pearly Gates on a VIP pass.

The first band went on and it turned out the singer was from Birmingham! You travel all the way across the world but you still can't escape the mind-numbing drawl that is the West Midlands' accent. But because he was English, he spoke us up for their entire set. I reckon we spent most of their set smiling and waving at staring locals.

I filled up my cup with beer and passed it to Maria.

"Thanks a lot for this. You *can* drive after one, can't you?"

Maria just smiled and took the beer.

Next up was us. We walked onstage and I don't think any of us took in a breath for the entire time. I must have lost about 20 lbs on that stage just through sheer adrenaline and energy. These three young idiots from the Isle of Wight had just walked into a major

Milwaukee music hole and given it a damn good pasting. It was awesome! The final show of the tour couldn't have gone any better. The sound was great and the crowd lapped it up. We all deserved a drink after that!

While the headline band played, Steve, Simon and I hit the bar and went milling around talking to the audience. They were all totally into what we did and it was a massive contrast from back home. There was no competition here. It was just about listening to music and having a good time.

Maria came over and asked for a beer. I figured she'd had one but that was a couple of hours ago and another one would still see her fit to drive. So I gave her my cup and she went off to get a pint.

The lads and I were all on separate sides of the room having different conversations and watching the band. When they'd finished and the building started emptying, we all found each other and grabbed one final beer for the road.

"Where's Maria?"

"No idea, mate. I haven't seen her since she came and asked me for a beer an hour ago."

"She took a beer off you?"

Oh, dear. It turned out that she hadn't just taken two pints from me. She'd taken two from Simon and two from Steve and now she was nowhere to be seen.

"She's had six pints? Fucking hell!" Six pints is a lot for a petite girl.

I sent a lady into the toilets to see if she was in there, and the girl appeared back pretty sharpish.

"You have to come see this."

The three of us crept into the ladies' toilets to find Maria. She was passed out with her head in the toilet. We all laughed at first until we realised that she was our ride home. It was well gone 1 am and we didn't have a clue how to get back to the hotel.

We carried her outside into the car park and tried to get her into her car. At this point, a big fellah started staggering across the car park towards us. All I could think about was how this would look to an outsider. Three English blokes trying to bundle a lifeless- looking girl into a car in the middle of the night doesn't sound that great, does it?

The bloke got closer, stopped and seemed to be assessing the situation. He looked at me and Simon holding an unconscious Maria. Then he looked at Steve, who was desperately trying to get into the car. Then a sentence of words came out of his mouth that I have never heard before or since:

"Don't you think it's funny that comic books are the only things that make you aware of Canada?"

What the fuck? We were frozen still. How do you respond to a line like that? We all looked at each other and the bloke staggered off.

If I was asked to suggest two billion potential lines that could have come out of that man's mouth, a line about comic books and Canada wouldn't have been one of them.

Steve managed to get in and we bundled Maria onto the back seat. Neither I nor Simon had driving licences, so Steve was handed the keys. We had been drinking, but at this point none of us felt drunk. A potential kidnapping in a foreign country tends to sober a man up.

"Where are we going?" "I have no fucking idea. Just drive."

So that's what we did. The streets were all deserted and so we drove aimlessly with absolutely no clue as to where we were going. None of us had paid any attention on the way there because we didn't foresee our driver getting battered and passing out. We must have been going around in circles looking for something we recognised for about 20 minutes. Just when things feel like they can't get any worse, they often do.

Steve was doing a great job of driving lost, on the wrong side of the road, in a foreign country and in a foreign car. But the powers-that-be weren't happy with our current predicament. They thought they'd throw in a police car. Y'know – just to mix it up a bit.

"Steve, we're being followed."

"Shit."

I was bricking it but trying to hold it together. The police car followed us for miles. We were the only two cars on the road and we could see the guy on his walkie-talkie thing. We figured that if he tried to trace the registration then we were fucked. Steve no longer wore make up and he certainly didn't look like a "Maria".

The copper put down his walkie-talkie thing and started to speed up. He hadn't put his blue light on yet but we figured it was only a matter of time. What the hell would they have thought of us? Three English lads, over the drink-drive limit, with no insurance, and the owner of the vehicle unconscious in the back. I think they'd have thrown an entire library of books at us.

"Look! The airport!"

Finally we'd spotted something we recognised. The hotel was just around the corner and in no time it was signposted. Thank God for that! We'd turn into the hotel and everything would be fine. We saw the sign and pulled in.

"Thank fuck for that!"

The police car followed us in to the Red Roof Inn car park. Now we were definitely for it. Steve pulled up outside the room and the three of us got out. By now the copper was parked up behind Maria's car. He didn't get out or say anything. He just shone a light directly at us.

"Steve, open the room door."

"What about Maria?"

"Fuck Maria, she can stay where she is for now!"

I wasn't about to bring a passed-out girl into the whole equation. The policeman didn't even know about her and already he had an issue with us.

Once in the room, we just stood there motionless. I was sure the copper would come banging on the door at any second. And once he did, we were fucked. Then we heard an engine start up and drive away. We opened the curtains and the police car had gone. How the hell did we get away with *that*?

The three of us dragged Maria into the hotel room and put her to bed. It looked like the three of us would be sharing a double bed that night. Although after that experience, not a lot of sleep was had.

Now, why was I mentioning the tea bags earlier? Well, when we returned from the tour, I was in need of a holiday – especially after our near brush with the law!

I ended up piling over to Amsterdam with a couple of old schoolmates. I just grabbed the same bag I'd taken to America, stuffed it full of clothes and headed off.

On the way back from Holland, we were stopped by French Customs and Excise. Now, because the coach was coming from Amsterdam, they dragged everyone off and searched through their belongings. A few people looked shifty, but I had no drugs and had gone there to drink and so I was pretty calm. That was until a guy dragged all my gear out and started shouting in French.

I took French at school and I was pretty good at it. But when you're being shouted at by a policeman it's slightly harder to understand. I don't think he was asking me where the patisserie was.

Another couple of officers came over and start ripping my clothes out and tossing them all over the place. Another officer came and stood behind me in case I tried to run. What the fuck? The first officer pulled his hand out and it was filled with what looked like cannabis leaves. I was shitting myself. Surely I hadn't been set up?!

They chatted in French for a bit and then they all started laughing. But not a nice friendly laugh. It was the kind of laugh that the evil villain does in a James Bond film.

So there I am, stood in a large queue of people all staring at me while I'm surrounded by police. And for some reason, they're all laughing at me.

"You fucking English and your tea," laughed the officer. He then bundled my stuff back in the bag and chucked it at me. What tea? Then the penny dropped. The Shivers and their bloody tea bags! They'd ended up splitting and spilling tea leaves all over the inside of my bag.

Cheers for that, guys. Some new underwear, please.

HOW NOT TO BE A ROCKSTAR

2: BREAKDOWNING STREET

London, 2004

Band members:
Gareth Icke - Vocals/Guitar
Tim Pritchard - Guitar
Turlough Ducie - Drums
Ollie Ducie - Bass
Taffy - Roadie/Driver

You know when you get those situations where you think "that could only ever happen to us"? Well, we were the kings of those situations. And this particular day was no different from any other.

I'm sure we probably attracted these things to ourselves, and a psychologist would have had an absolute field day with our thought projections. Truth was, if it got to about 5 pm and nothing bizarre had happened, we'd be looking at each other confused.

"Why is one of us not bleeding?"

We'd all taken the great leap and moved up to London. As much as we loved our Isle of Wight heritage, the management thought it might be better if we embraced London a bit more. This meant having various photo shoots in and around recognisable London landmarks. They thought that we should be a little bit trendier in order to fit in with the London "scene". I must admit, that was a bit odd for us given that we'd spent the last 10 years of our lives trying to achieve the opposite.

We felt we'd found our "trendy" by being completely "untrendy" – but apparently not. That's the thing about the music industry in general – it's all so superficial. Punk rock, to me growing up, was a way of expressing your true identity. But truthfully, it isn't at all. It's a label, like every other label, and it's a fashion as much as it is an art. In fact, the art- to-fashion ratio is weighted heavily in the favour of the image.

It was a sunny afternoon in February or March and we were on our way into Central London for a photo shoot in Covent Garden. It was the perfect day for it. Covent Garden was packed with tourists – mostly foreign – and so it would be great way of spreading the name "Kody" around as well as getting a few cool photos. We were very much, in our minds at least, a "band of the people", so random images in crowds were always cool

with us. Better than the cliché images such as standing next to a road sign saying something like "Last Exit". I know some people think that's profound. It's not. It's just a road sign.

Our manager, Gary, had a friend that owned a photography studio inside Covent Garden itself. He was a talented photographer but, like most people that move to London to chase their dream, he'd ended up where the money was. And in a tourist trap like that, it was taking cheesy shots of people dressed up in Olde English dresses and top hats. The foreigners loved it, and he needed the money.

That very situation is what terrified us about moving to London in the first place. I had so many friends that had made the move to follow their dream as a musician or an artist. To be fair, there are more opportunities in the big cities. But what they fail to tell you is that there is also another million people vying for said opportunities. In the end, my friends ended up working two or three jobs just to pay the rent, while their dream took a back seat. They always said it would be just until they became established, but, 10 years later, the dream had died to be replaced with a mortgage and a second-hand Renault Clio.

"We all have to grow up someday y'know, Gareth." I wish I had a pound for every time I've heard that. I was never fully sure of whether they were trying to make me believe that or whether they were just trying to reassure themselves that they'd made the right choices in life. Probably the latter, I suspect.

Anyway, I can't remember the photographer's name, which is pretty bad of me. I think it was Terry or something like that. Let's just pretend anyway. For the story, we'll call him Terry. He was about 45 or so. A nice bloke actually, and he liked a beer which is always a bonus. It was a conversation-starter at least. Most conversations we had with him started with the line, "What you having?" But that worked for us.

The plan was simple – Terry would reel off tonnes of random photos and we'd just have to stand about looking cool and attracting attention while our management handed out flyers to people that looked interested. It doesn't matter who you are or what you look like, point a camera at you and people come flocking. Terry managed to get a few decent shots, but mostly we ended up just posing for pictures with Japanese tourists.

"I send pictures back home and tell friends we met Kody, yes?" I'm not very good at accents.

It's always quite nice to feel famous and successful for a day, but the truth was they didn't have a bloody clue who we were. And whoever opened up that email back in Japan and saw the photos wouldn't know who the bloody hell we were either. That's the hilarious thing about so-called "celebrity". All these people wanted photographs and things signing, but they had never heard a song or even heard the name before. It was

all just the perception of fame and success. Again, a behavioural psychologist could probably have a real blast with these people.

I've been asked if I'm famous a bunch of times. My answer is always the same: "Clearly not."

In future, if ever I get lonely and need an ego boost, I might just pay someone a fiver to take pictures of me to attract attention. I'll make it slightly more interesting for the tourists though. When asked who I am, I'll affect an accent and say I'm an escaped war criminal from the Middle East.

"We're just taking some pictures to send back to the victims' families." What is so tragic is I bet people would still pose for pictures with me.

"Here's me at the London Eye ... Here's me with David Beckham at Madame Tussauds ... and here's me with a very friendly man who firebombed a village school."

So yeah, we spent the morning walking around having photos taken with various people and next to various things. But I've told you enough stories for you to know where this one will inevitably lead. That's right – the pub. We lads were quite the fans of Covent Garden generally, and tended to spend a fair bit of our free time there. We were all pretty skint in those days and it was basically a source of free entertainment. There was always someone performing magic, playing music or just doing something odd with a unicycle and a set of knives. All that aside, the real entertainment always came from watching the general public. The things people do when they don't realise anyone is watching. A lot of it is certifiable. And so all we'd really need is a couple of beers and we'd be set for an entire day of "people watching".

My dad always said that there are three types of people: the doers, the followers and the ones who run around wondering what's going on. I'd always liked to consider myself a doing person, but at times it's actually nice to take a rest and watch people being people.

There was a pub in Covent Garden called The Punch & Judy. It wasn't cheap, but if we did have a couple of quid it was our pub of choice. It had a seating area outside that was perfect to spy on fat American tourists wrestling with their "UNIVERSAL STUDIOS – FLORIDA" fanny packs. After a couple of hours of being the centre of attention, we were all ready to chill out with a beer and watch other people for a bit.

And so, as always, a beer turned into two and three and four, and in no time Taffy and Gary were responsible for four drunken musicians and a half-cut photographer. You'd think we'd have got bored of drinking, wouldn't you? I think deep inside we were all waiting for the day when someone would ask us what we were having, something would click in our brain and we'd order an orange juice. That day never came. I think a couple of us still harbour that thought to this day. Truth is, it's never going to happen. We are what we are and the NHS will just have to suck it up and deal with it.

Taffy and Gary were sober and bored and angling for us to leave. So the load of us stocked up on beer from the off-licence and piled back into the bus. I'm not sure how far we lived from the centre of London. As the crow flies it was probably just a half-hour journey. But this is London, and you get nowhere fast. With the traffic and the one-way systems and all the other nonsense, it would take us a good couple of hours to get home to East Molesey. That's where the crate of beer would come in. See, drinking in those days was very much like opening a pack of Pringles – once you'd popped, there was no stopping, at least until you were either asleep, or dead.

Taffy started up the bus and we cracked open the Carlsberg. Obviously we'd had a few weird moments with the Japanese tourists, but none of them really constituted a "You Have" moment. And as I said earlier, if we hadn't had a bizarre happening by around 5 pm, we'd start asking questions. It was probably about three in the afternoon and the 5 pm weirdness-deadline was fast approaching.

Everyone was secretly thinking it but not wanting to tempt fate. Then there came an ominous clunking sound from the bus's engine, and Taffy started to lose control.

"Ahhh, and there we have it!" we all thought. When everything is running smoothly, that's when you should worry, because it's only a matter of time before the shit hits the fan belt.

It turns out there was a big problem with the clutch and Taffy was fighting to even get the bus to move. If we stopped at a red light we'd be screwed, so the mission was to drive as slowly as possible and not stop. If a light went red, we'd just coast towards it and hope to God it went green again before we actually came to a standstill. This worked for a while, but there was no way in hell we were getting all the way back to Lance's place without assistance.

In Central London there is a strict zero-compassion policy on anyone who breaks down. You could be a 90-year-old war veteran with smoke billowing out of the bonnet of your Morris Minor and they'd still slap a ticket on your windscreen.

"I know you thought you fought for our freedom, but that freedom allows me to give you an on-the-spot fine."

So, here we were in a no-win situation. There was no way we were getting back to Surrey, and there was no way we could afford to break down on double red lines. A very loose plan was hatched. Pray to the Lord of Ford Transit and cross our fingers that the bus would keep going long enough to get us out of the city centre.

As luck would have it, we managed to keep going just long enough to break down in Whitehall, right outside Downing Street – the home of the Prime Minister. The van coughed and spluttered a fair bit and then shuddered to a halt right outside the gates. We honestly couldn't have planned it better if we'd tried.

The van was surrounded by police in no time. Terrorism is thrust into people's faces on a daily basis, and one thing the police tend to get concerned about is a massive van full of drunken bearded blokes parked directly outside the home of the country's prime minister.

We were all drunk in the back, and finding it pretty funny to be honest. There was nothing we could do about it. The van was buggered and none of us had the first clue about how to fix it. The police could shout and bark orders as much as they wanted; it wasn't going to change anything. This bus was going nowhere.

A couple of coppers climbed inside and one of them tried to start the bus. The other police officer came into the back to talk to us.

"They give you magical powers when you join the police force, mate?"

"I'm sorry?"

"Because your mate's going to need them if he thinks he's starting this thing."

The van wouldn't start for the magical policeman, so that bought us some time. At least they knew we weren't faking it. Plus, after a minute-long conversation with us, the second officer realised we were probably incapable of blowing up a balloon, let alone a government building.

Taffy got on the phone to The AA for some breakdown assistance and we carried on drinking. They were sending a truck to pick us up, and that seemed to be enough to keep the police off our backs for a while.

While we were sitting there, these two older ladies stopped to stare at the bus. I thought they were just being nosey, but it turned out they were from the Isle of Wight and had recognised the band name from the side of the bus. Turlough invited them both on board.

"So, which one's Keith Chegwin's son?" asked the older one.

"Me, but it isn't Keith Chegwin. I don't think so, anyway," I replied.

We offered them both a beer and they accepted gladly. They were in town to watch the singer from Crowded House play a solo show. I forget his name. Neil Flynn, or something? Anyway, they were in a similar frame of mind to us and were happy to guzzle the beers. I think that's a small-town thing. Every trip out of your tight-knit community constitutes a holiday in our minds. And when on holiday, anything goes. What we hadn't taken into consideration was the fact that we were no longer on holiday and we actually lived here now.

So, we had a few beers with the lovely ladies and waited patiently for the AA recovery truck to come and save us. Only problem was, when it turned up, the AA vehicle was actually smaller than our bus. This kind of thing only happens to us.

While the AA man was there, he took a look at the bus to see if it could be fixed by the side of the road. Anything would do, as long as it could get us out of this mess. We'd gladly take the fine now.

After about 30 seconds of fiddling around under the bonnet, he popped his head into the bus.

"Yeah, it's fucked."

"Is that your expert opinion?"

We'd have to call for another, much bigger pick-up truck. But by the time we'd got to this point, we'd been stuck there for a while and the patience was starting to wear thin with the Downing Street security.

There was one guy who looked more like a terrorist than an anti-terrorist. He kept pacing up and down alongside the bus, talking on a walkie-talkie for a bit, shouting at someone to do something, then back to pacing. You could see he was getting more and more agitated with our presence. But what the hell were we meant to do? We'd done everything they'd asked of us. It wasn't our fault that the AA didn't know their arses from their elbows.

Then, chaos ensued. The terrorist-looking bloke started barking orders and various police officers started running towards our bus.

"Shit lads, this doesn't look good."

One police officer called for all of us to get out of the bus. It was like something you'd expect to see in Israel or Kosovo – not in the streets of London. Were they going to line us up against the wall and shoot us or something? When you have that many different people shouting different things it's hard to make sense of anything. The scary terrorist- looking bloke came bounding over.

"Right, we need to move this van and we need to move it now. We have a very important diplomat arriving shortly and we simply can't have this vehicle here."

Well that was all well and good, but exactly how he planned to move the thing was as yet unexplained.

"Who's the lightest? Right you, skinny bloke, you're steering."

"Me?" I said holding my beer aloft.

"Yes, you. You are in control of steering and everyone else can push."

"Couple of things, Officer ... one, I'm pissed; and two, I don't actually have a driving licence."

"You are steering."

Now call me paranoid, but isn't that illegal? Now, my trust in the police doesn't extend too far and so I assumed it was just an elaborate way to get me arrested.

"Excuse me, Officer, but if I take control of this van, are you not just going to do me for drink driving ... without a licence?"

He went on to explain that in exceptional circumstances such as this, sometimes rules needed to be broken to resolve the situation. Exceptional circumstances?! I was unaware that a van breaking down could be considered exceptional.

And so I asked him: "Exceptional circumstances?"

"Would you like to take a look up there, Sir?"

He pointed to the roof of the building opposite and at two or three snipers on top – their rifles pointing directly at us. I had to ask, didn't I?!

"I'll steer then?"

"Probably best."

I climbed into the driving seat with the can of beer still in my hand, and released the handbrake. Tim, Taffy, Turlough, Ollie, Gary and a couple of policemen were pushing the bus while I steered, and the scary terror-officer ran alongside shouting directions at me. I figured by this point that I should probably just laugh about it. After all, it's not every day that you get sniper rifles pointed at you. So every time we'd pass a group of tourists, I'd press the horn and raise my can to them. This obviously attracted a hell of a lot of attention and photographs. The difference was, these ones would actually interest their friends back home.

"Here's me at Big Ben ... Here's me at Tower Bridge ... Here's a drunken guy raising his beer to me as he's driving a van while a group of policemen push it down the road."

Once we were out of the way, I whacked the handbrake back on and waited for the repercussions. There were none. Surely they were going to at least tell me off for honking the horn. But, nothing. They just said, "Cheers, lads", and left us there. And that was that. We were no nearer to actually getting home, but we *were* nearer to a Sainsbury's. Which was a blessing, really. Having a gun pointed at you sure does make you hungry.

3: FLY BY NIGHT

Isle of Wight, 2004

Band members:
Gareth Icke - Vocals/Guitar
Tim Pritchard - Guitar
Turlough Ducie - Drums
Steve Richmond - Bass
Dan Hill - DJ/Keys

So, we had ourselves a manager at last. It was something we'd been in desperate need of for a fair while. I could write the songs, the lads could then make them sound a hell of a lot better, and we could perform them live. That bit was nailed. We had no issues with that. What we didn't have, however, was the business knowledge that went along with it.

The first mission we were set was to conquer the Isle of Wight. Not just our local venue or the odd mini-festival, but the entire island. All 150,000 people had to know who we were. Be they grandmothers or teenagers, the plan was to get enough exposure and have enough local column inches to guarantee we were a household name. Once we'd managed that, we'd have enough local backing and support to go on to take on the bigger fish in London and beyond.

Our manager, James, was all about the "Big Show". In his mind, the band had played enough gigs and we should therefore be concentrating our efforts on bigger, better shows – but play less often. So instead of walking into The Squadron, for instance, and catching a Kody gig, it would be more of an event – something that the local radio and press could get behind. It annoyed us at the time because all we wanted to do was gig. I was writing so many songs, and, without even ever performing them, many were replaced by newer songs. But, like I said, we didn't have a business brain like James did. This was a guy that would hand out a thousand VIP tickets for a venue that only held 300 people. That would ensure that the queue went round the block and that people were turned away. It's all about perception. The following weeks would bring out even more people to see what the fuss was about. This guy was a pro, and we trusted his judgement.

There was a big theatre in Shanklin called The Portico. Every six months or so we'd play a big show there and share the proceeds. The profit was divided amongst the bands and

Pete, the Portico's manager. Pete would put his share towards fixing the roof or whatever else needed doing to keep the place ticking along. It was quite weird really as the venue itself was relatively modern but had been allowed to fall into a state of disrepair. You don't normally find that with buildings that are only 20-odd years old. Mind you, it was in a very wealthy area of the island and the value of the land alone would have been astronomical. I would imagine the Council was rubbing its hands together at the prospect of the owner running out of funds and the theatre finally crumbling. I'm sure that's why, over the years, they did nothing to help its survival in terms of grants. As it happens, years later, it was levelled, and now it's a rather swanky housing estate. I guess they got their wish – not that I'm cynical or anything.

Our next show at the Portico was just a few weeks away, and James had decided that this was perfect for our first "Big Show". We'd already booked up bands that we knew had quite a following on the Island, so we were pretty much guaranteed a good turnout without much in the way of advertising. We spoke to the local radio station and to the local newspaper and both had run small but positive pieces on the event. In our small musical minds, we'd done enough to promote the show and now we just had to rehearse hard and make sure the performance was up to scratch. Simple.

The five of us and James used to meet up once a week at a local café/bar called Joe Daflo's. It was a cool, trendy place that was once owned by Mark King from the band Level 42. The lot of us would sink some beers and brainstorm a few ideas about where we felt we should take the band. Most of the ideas were lost in the ensuing drunkenness and replaced by off-the-planet schemes that can only have been put down to 5% lager.

I remember one idea was a music video for our song *Black and*

White Photography. We felt, whilst drunk, that the best way to portray a song I wrote about myself and my own shortcomings was to fly to Romania and film with some orphans. I think it even went so far as to have us in colour and the orphans in black and white – a bloody awful idea that would have offended probably more people than it amused. You get the point though? Ninety-nine per cent of these ideas were laughed off in the morning and never revisited. Except for one.

James had suggested we do a bit of fly-posting around the island. We were already one step ahead. We'd made up some A4-sized posters and put them up around town, on closed-down shops and on the odd smashed-up bus shelter. But no, this wasn't anything like close to what James had planned. He was talking A1-sized billboard-style posters all over everything and everyone. If a homeless man was asleep, he'd awaken to find himself covered in a Kody poster. No stone was to be left unturned, no village noticeboard uncovered. He wanted people to talk about this for days.

When we woke up nursing our hangovers, we all assumed it was the beer talking and that there was no way he could be serious. After all, this was highly illegal and none of us had the money to pay the fine. Plus, unlike a piece of graffiti that says "all coppers are bastards", this would have our name on it. And not only that, but it would tell the police exactly where we were going to be at a certain time on a certain day.

My phone rang.

"Hello?"

"Hey, Gareth, it's James. You sewer rats sorted out the posters and paste yet? We're on it tonight."

It would take too long to explain why he called us sewer rats – mainly because I'm not entirely sure myself. But he did, and he was serious about pasting the Isle of Wight into one big _neon_ Kody poster. Did I not mention that part? Oh, yeah, the posters were to be illuminous yellow – bright enough for even an elderly woman with cataracts to read.

Turlough and Tim took care of the posters, and Dan Hill and Steve got hold of the paste. We were ready to go. Now all we needed to do was wait until it was dark. James would be driving one car and Dan Hill would be driving the other. The rest of us hit the pub. If we were going to be defacing people's property at 1 am, then we'd rather be doing it with the aid of some dutch courage.

The time came and we all drove out to paint the town neon. We covered every single town on the Isle of Wight. It took us hours, and by the time we were done the sun was rising. Two hundred and fifty A1-sized bright-yellow posters had covered everything in sight. We covered every council billboard, every disused shop front, every telephone box and pillar box, and we plastered one above every cash machine. Nothing was safe from the poster and the paste.

Time was getting on, and we figured that at any moment somebody would wake up and alert the police. When they did, we didn't want to be sat in a car surrounded by posters and covered in paste. We'd planned to be tucked up in bed when that first patrol vehicle spotted what we'd done. The final town was Newport, the island's capital, and James had certainly saved the best until last.

On weekdays from 1 pm to 2 pm, Isle of Wight Radio used to broadcast the Alex Dyke Phone-In. Now, Alex was a top bloke who always looked after us by playing our music and selling us over the radio. But he was also the king of the wind-up. The phone-in attracted up to a million listeners, and no-one knew what he was going to say and who he was going to offend. It was all completely tongue-in-cheek, of course; but, on the whole, people are pretty dim when it comes to spotting sarcasm.

James's plan was to plaster the entire front windows of Isle of Wight Radio's premises with posters. This would ensure that our show was at the top of Alex Dyke's agenda come phone-in time. We pulled up and Turlough and I crept up to the windows. The studio was in a business park just off the island's only dual carriageway. We'd have to be pretty damn quick and back on the road to Ryde as soon as possible. Whatever posters we had left went on the building. No-one would be able to miss them when they arrived at work.

Once the posters were up, we dived into the car and made our way back. It must have been around 4 am by the time we got home. Add the time to the beer and all the running around we'd done, and sleeping was not an issue.

I'd booked the following day off work because I was certain that the previous evening's antics would go on to an ungodly hour. I wasn't wrong, and was actually quite excited about spending a much-needed day in bed. It wasn't to be though as my phone was ringing off the hook. Isle of Wight Radio had gone ballistic.

It was all anyone on the Island was talking about. People were phoning in even before the phone-in had started, all of them saying the same thing about how outraged they were that someone had done this. It didn't bother us though because it was having the desired effect. The more of the Isle of Wight's older generation that called in to voice their anger at these "young hooligans", the more that the younger generation got behind it. Ticket sales were going through the roof and everything was going to plan. It would take two minutes to rip down a poster, but it would take a hell of a lot longer than that to get the name "Kody" out of people's heads. And now, because we appeared to be a lot more anti-authority, we'd managed to win over a load more young people that had thought we weren't punk rock enough. We didn't dress punk, you see. To some people, it's all in the appearance.

The five of us were all sat in the Solent Inn with the radio on. The Alex Dyke Phone-In was in full swing and the people weren't letting up with their ranting. We were public enemy number one, but only among a demographic that we weren't bothered about. These people were never going to buy our records or come to our shows. But they kept our name on the radio, and for that we were very grateful. But then like all risqué schemes, someone always bottles it and wrecks the plan for everyone else.

Alex was bigging up how angry he was and how he couldn't believe someone had done such a thing. It was all done on purpose to get listeners phoning in. The truth was, Alex was rock 'n' roll through-and-through and couldn't give a shit that someone had plastered the station. In fact, he probably clapped his hands in private to a great marketing campaign. At one point, he even cleared our name and said that it must have been one of the other bands on the bill because we weren't capable of doing it. He said that we were top lads who were regularly supported by Isle of Wight Radio. There was no way that we'd bite the hand that fed us. That was the only moment I felt in any way guilty.

Then came the phone call – the owner of the Portico Theatre. Not our friend, Pete, who ran the place, but a silent owner that nobody actually knew. He called up to say he was pulling the gig. What the fuck?! The guy's venue was falling down and we'd just sold more tickets than he could have dreamed of. And now he was going to pull the show?! Was the guy insane?!

Alex Dyke's reaction was exactly the same as ours.

"No, don't do that. There is no need to do that!"

But the owner wouldn't budge. He didn't want his venue to have the bad publicity and that was that. What he failed to realise was that without shows like ours, he wouldn't have a venue left to protect from bad publicity.

Alex thought on his feet and cut a deal.

"If whoever is responsible comes down here, apologises, and takes down the posters, then the gig will go ahead and we'll give it our full support. How's that?"

The owner agreed, and so the show was back on. But with one condition of course. We sat around looking at each other. We were in a no-win situation. If we went and apologised, the gig would go ahead but there was no way we would get played on Isle of Wight Radio again. And, on the other hand, if we didn't go and apologise, the gig would be pulled after all the effort we'd put into it.

"Well, we'll lose any rock 'n' roll credibility we've got if we apologise. Can you imagine Keith Moon saying "Sorry" for putting up some posters? It wouldn't happen."

We were absolutely pinned between a rock and a very hard place. We ordered another round of beers and got thinking. No matter what ideas any of us had, it would always end up with one of the above. The band would end up losing out no matter what.

The radio phone-in had taken the role of background noise by now. There are only so many middle-aged rants you can listen to before they all start blending into one. Then, Alex interrupted a caller to state that the situation had been resolved. A young lad had gone down to Isle of Wight Radio and apologised for putting up the posters. He'd then gone so far as to tear down the posters and clean the paste off the windows. Alex exclaimed that the culprit had come clean, and because of that the show would go ahead. This was excellent news, and we were all happy that the show was saved, but at the same time we were all a fair bit confused. The *culprit* hadn't apologised and torn down the posters. The culprits were all sat around the bar of the Solent Inn nursing Kronenbourgs. So who on earth was this lad? We never ever found out who that kid was. And believe me, we asked around for a long time. But even to this day, I have no idea who the kid was. We owe him a pretty damn big thank-you, too. He saved our arses!

The show itself was a belter. It was a complete sell-out, and the Portico Theatre made a fair few quid to help towards its upkeep. Everyone was a winner. The venue made some money, the bands got some much needed exposure and our set even ended up with a massive stage invasion. Nothing makes you feel more of a rock star than a giant stage

invasion. This was our first step towards conquering our Island, and completing step one of James's management plan.

After our set was done, the five of us were on a huge high – the kind of adrenaline buzz that can only come about through stage invasions or Class A narcotics. And since none of us were into drugs, the stage invasion would have to be our heroin. None of us could believe just how much the plan had worked. Just a few posters had caused such a stir on our little island that we became a household name. We'd angered adults and attracted the youth. It was a plan that Simon Cowell would have been proud of. James, however, didn't bat an eyelid. He just stood there at the back with a wry smile on his face. Kody was a project, and Rome wasn't built in a day; but with a few neon bits of paper and some paste, we'd built a rather fetching foundation.

4: THE "YOU HAVE" TOUR

England, 2004

Band members:
Gareth Icke - Vocals/Guitar
Tim Pritchard - Guitar
Turlough Ducie - Drums
Steve Richmond - Bass
Taffy - Roadie/Driver

Right ... the *You Have* tour. What a crazy month that was! I think I've spent the years since actually trying to make sense of all the madness. I'll start at the beginning.

First of all, I'll explain the name. I'm sure I've told you this already, but I'll risk repeating myself. Just go with it. Basically, if something out of the ordinary happened, such as a man falling over, or a very-drunk girl talking nonsense, or whatever, we'd say, "You have". It was a way of saying, "You've got that pissed-up idiot written all over you", but without the backlash that would come from calling someone a pissed-up idiot directly. I learned the hard way and so it was shortened to "You have". So that's the name explained. Sort of.

We were living on the Isle of Wight, practising constantly, but not really playing that many shows. We knew that we couldn't gig on our island all the time, because you'd just get overkill. We decided that a big show every few months would be a much better way to go. And it was. The only problem was, we were bored. We'd formed a band to play shows. Live performances were sort of the point.

We'd talked about touring and stuff, and we'd often do a couple of days here and there – but nothing like a proper rock 'n' roll tour. Growing up in a small town tends to give you a small-town mentality. As much as you try to fight it, it still manages to seep in a little bit.

The Isle of Wight was comfortable. We all had long-term girlfriends; we all had jobs and flats of our own; and we all had our local pub. When life is comfortable, it's a lot harder to motivate yourself to live in a bus in the freezing cold.

Then one morning, my girlfriend told me she was going to Spain for a couple of months. "Eh?" Isn't that something you discuss as a couple? But she needed to get away and that was fair enough. The only problem was, I wasn't that great at being alone in those days. Plus, I didn't really like the idea of being reminded of my absent girlfriend at every turn. Small towns are like that. Everything and everyone will somehow link back to her.

My "comfort" was now gone, and so the freezing-cold van didn't seem that bad. I figured if I was off gigging in Newcastle-upon-Tyne, I wouldn't be bumping into people asking, "How is she getting on in Spain?"

It sounds like I'm being immature. But the truth is, I really loved that girl and missed her like a severed limb. I wasn't a "real" man back then – I had emotions and everything. I also owned two copies of _Dirty Dancing_, but that's not the point.

Taffy and his girlfriend had just split up around the same time, so he was also game for an escapism road trip. The others really didn't need much persuading, to be honest. The idea was born. In a month, we'd hit the road for 28 days solid.

Most tours take months and months of preparation, but, like everything we did in those days, we figured we'd blag it. We picked the dates and got on the phone. The idea was kind of to map out a route, but with such short notice it was also a case of take what we could get. Some shows would pay cash, some would pay in booze and some would just make us feel uncomfortable. But that was all part of the fun, I suppose. Five mates all thrust into some bizarre scenarios, hundreds of miles from home.

I was having a fair bit of luck on the phone, especially with the venues in and around the Midlands, in England. I am originally from that part of the world, and I have family there. Once you tell a promoter that you can guarantee people through the door, they'll always give you a slot. They can hear the "kerching!" of the tills. The other lads weren't having so much luck. Tim had managed to get a couple of shows in the west of England, but they were more favours from mates and so didn't pay. In the end, we had to draft Turlough's brother, Ollie, in to help. He'd toured a fair bit and had the gift of the gab when it came to talking to promoters.

We'd sit down in front of the computer and search for live venues in a certain area, and then get on the phone. Most pubs and clubs wanted cover-bands, which was us out of the window of course. We must have made about 200 phone calls to get those 28 shows. We did have a laugh doing it though. After a couple of hours of booking and drinking beer, we'd always get a little bored and stupid.

"Hello, Travellers Rest."

"Do you spew live mule-sick at halls?"

"I'm sorry?"

"Do you do live music at all?"

"Oh! I thought you said something about a mule's sick!"

"Must be a bad line."

One conversation had me in stitches. It's probably not even that funny right now but, at the time, and after a few beers, it was. Our mate, Jules, had got in on the action; he was pretending to be our agent and called up a venue up north. They blatantly wanted a cover band but Jules wasn't giving up on it.

"We really need some covers to be honest, lad."

"They do *Horse With No Name* by America."

(We didn't, by the way.)

"Oh, okay. What else do they do?"

"I'll tell you what they *do* cover brilliantly."

"Yeah?"

"America."

"What? Like a tribute?"

"They play *Horse With No Name*."

I don't know where Jules had got this obsession from. We'd never played that song and none of us even liked it that much. It was just one of those old songs everyone knew because it was on every crap compilation that had ever been given away with a newspaper.

Needless to say, the landlord wasn't interested and that venue would not be booking us.

Over the next week or so, we blagged and blagged more and more shows. Some of the venue owners we lied to, and some of them genuinely loved what we were doing. Some were actually awesome shows at venues we'd played before and had earned us a following. Whatever happened, it was going to be very boozy and very messy. But we figured that we wouldn't be doing this when we were 45, so we may as well do it now. What we hadn't considered is that we'd probably be dead before we got near to 45. When you're young, the future is just something grown-ups worry about, right?

Everyone on the Isle of Wight got behind us, and people were really excited about what we were doing. I'll be honest – our island has plenty of jealous, nasty people that would sooner pull their neighbours down than ever assist them in anything. That's just how the place works. If someone is doing anything out of the ordinary, it often hurts people. It makes them reflect on their own mundane lives, and no-one likes to do that. So they rain on your parade. So for people to actually be behind us was incredible. I'm not talking about our group of friends – they're good people and were always behind us. I'm talking about the wider community.

The local radio station was playing our music and talking about the tour. Our local newspaper ran a half-page story about it. People we didn't know were even stopping us in the street and wishing us good luck. It was great. But most of all, the people in our local pub were incredible.

The night before the tour began, we all headed to The Solent for some farewell beers. As you can imagine, a few beers turned in to a full-on session. The landlord, Andy, came downstairs with a massive crate of beer and a hundred pounds. He kept saying, "This is the beginning. This has to go well." I understood how the £100 would help it go well. It would go straight into the fuel tank. But I wasn't sure how that many cans of Kronenbourg would do anything but fuel our already spiraling alcohol problems!

Then our friend, Henry, came in for a beer. Henry had been a local legend for years and his sons, Rich and Pete, were in our group of friends. He also owned the shop next door to the pub. He handed over a hundred quid and a crate of German lager. We knew the month was going to be messy, but it was appearing to be looking messier by the minute.

The following morning, we were all up bright and early. First night of the tour was in Royal Leamington Spa. It's a beautiful Roman town in the English West Midlands. It is also my town of birth so it felt like a good place to start the tour. And there would be family and friends there, which is always a bonus. The only problem was that Leamington Spa was about a three-and-a-half-hour drive, and we'd also need to go via London to drop off our mate, Stuart. Hence the early start.

Normally, an early wake-up call would be fine, but with us it meant we were all still really hungover. Add that to the fact that we were all firm believers in the "hair of the dog" hangover cure (another beer). Then, multiply that by the two giant crates of beer we had just loaded into the bus. The recipe is quite simply for disaster. Tim's mum and dad dropped him off with all his gear, only to see me, Steve and Turlough in the back, tucking into beers at 7 am. Their faces dropped. What were they letting their son in for?

We were basically just topping up the beer from the night before, so after a couple of cans we were right back to being drunk again. When you get on the 8 am ferry drunk, people tend to look at you in a very confused way. But then we were a punk rock band – what were they expecting? Once on the boat we were the subject of everyone's attention. Four drunken guys, a Welshman in leathers, and our mate, Stuart, who was basically a Liam Gallagher clone.

I was already stumbling a little bit, and the tuts and arm-folds were apparent in many of the passengers. But then a small child shouted out, "Mummy! That's Kody!" And the mother came over and asked if we'd have a photo taken with her son. Obviously we obliged, and they went to sit back down.

Now, I have a confession: that kid only knew who we were because we would occasionally go (sober) into primary schools and middle schools across the Isle of Wight
to play charity shows for the kids. But as far as the rest of the passengers were concerned, we were clearly famous. It's amazing how people's attitudes change when they think they're dealing with celebrity. Like if a guy is drunk at 8 am, he's an alcoholic loser; but if a famous musician is smashed at 8 am, he's cool and rock 'n' roll. What's the difference? There *is* no difference. But we all found it hilarious.

In fact, at one point on the journey I popped into the Gents and a guy said to me:

"Oi, mate. Are you famous?"

"Umm ... clearly not," was my reply. If you have to ask someone if they're famous – they aren't.

We managed to skull another couple of beers on the hour-long boat ride. We ended up sat next to this big group of tourists. They were a good laugh and had clearly been on the Island for some kind of piss-up. *They* weren't going to judge. I noticed that one of the women was reading the County Press. It was our local paper and was normally full of "cat stuck up tree" stories. They'd always manage to keep the drug stories out of the paper. It was a tourist island after all ... can't be scaring away the old folks and their hard-earned pension money.

I asked the lady what was on the cover of the Entertainment section.

"How come?"

"Just wondered."

She spent ages wrestling with this massive broadsheet paper before finally finding the Entertainment part. As she opened, it there was a huge photo of us lot. When she glanced back at us, with a look of "you arrogant tossers" on her face, we were re- creating the pose.

They realised we were taking the piss out of ourselves and we all had a good laugh. I can't remember what the pose was but it was probably really cliché and moody. I don't know why we did that. On stage we took the piss and had a laugh, yet in photos we always tried to be smouldering. It was probably to get girls. It didn't work.

Once we were on the mainland, we were straight up the motorway to London and straight back into the crate of beer. It wasn't even 10 am and we were all completely battered. We had a show that night but figured we'd just have a nap before we played and everything would be fine.

Taffy was heading to Surbiton to meet Stuart's dad and drop Stuart off there. When we arrived, we were all so drunk that we needed food if we were going to last until the show. Right around the corner from the railway station is a McDonald's. Now normally I won't eat that shit, but I was drunk and starving. This is where it all got a bit messy. I queued up for ages, ordered my meal, waited patiently – if a little wobbly – for it to be

served. I thanked the girl, turned around and then boom! I'd smashed straight into some bloke – burger, chips and Coca-Cola everywhere. I turned to the shell-shocked young girl, smiled, and said, "A Big Mac meal please."

That was money well spent.

After we'd all eaten what can only be described as manure in a bun, we piled back into the bus and headed out of London. Now this was a dark moment for me. I skulled a can of beer and then, while sat between Turlough and Steve, I sharted. Now a "shart" is neither a fart nor a shit. But it is, unfortunately, a combination of the two. So there I am, sat in a tour bus, surrounded by my mates, and I've just unloaded a little bit of shit into my pants. Was that all part of the rock 'n' roll lifestyle as well? Because I hadn't signed up for that part.

"Taffy! Can you stop at the next service station please, mate? I've just shit myself."

After a clean-up, underwear change and a few more beers, we arrived in Leamington Spa. I hadn't been up this way for a fair while and it had seriously changed. I mean, for instance, the last time I was there, an open-top Mercedes full of Indians hadn't shouted "faggot!" at me. But then I suppose I wasn't wearing a bright-pink headband and a pink studded belt with a glittery "G" on it back then. People feel uncomfortable around pink studded belts.

The venue was down by the railway arches. It was called "Kelly's" and it seemed to have a very loose Irish theme. When I say loose, I basically mean it wasn't Irish at all. But Irish people drink heavily and are famous for it. I guess they figured if it had a couple of shamrocks on the wall, it might be able to tap into that lucrative Irish booze-culture. It was a bit cramped, but nice enough. Plus, cramped venues are always good because they tend to look busier than they actually are. We'd learned that by playing massive venues with no bugger in them!

Turlough nudged me. "Have you seen the wall display?"

There was a massive chalkboard, and on it in brightly coloured writing it said "THE KODIES ROCK SHOW!!!" and there was a picture of a steel Dire-Straits-style guitar.

"Oh, dear."

The turnout for our opening night was pretty good. There was a fair few people there but, with the exception of my family members, they were all looking for "The Kodies Rock Show". I would imagine the Kodies would play *Horse With No Name* by America.

So, we played our first set and it went down okay. You could see that a few of the audience were disappointed that there weren't any covers. But on the whole it was all right. Then, the landlord comes over and asks us could we play covers in the second set – just to keep the locals happy. Well, we were in a Catch 22 situation because a) we didn't know any covers, and b) if the audience didn't stick around and buy beer, the

landlord wasn't going to pay us. So, we just agreed to play some covers and got back up on the stage. What the hell were we going to do? I looked down at the set-list and then looked at Tim. He thought on his feet. Tim had moments of genius occasionally.

"This is an old Deep Purple B-side. It's not that well known, but we're massive fans."

Then we cracked out one of our own. The crowd loved it. They were cheering, and the landlord gave us the thumbs-up. Were they honestly that bloody stupid? Yes, yes they were. We kept that up all night. We played old "Led Zeppelin" songs from rare Japanese releases; "Cream" songs that were never fully distributed because of a record-company wrangle. You name it – we made it up and then played a song of our own. Everyone was having an absolute blast. But what made me laugh was when we got to the final song, and we said, "This is one of our own", and there were audible groans from the audience. Were these guys for real?

I think it was just a roomful of mid-life crises. These leather-jacket-wearing fellahs were probably estate agents six months ago. Then, a daughter called one of them her "old man" in a phone conversation with her boyfriend; he overheard, bought a leather jacket and a Harley Davidson, and started taking the wife to Kelly's. They knew sod all about music but they knew a few classic 70s and 80s band names. They wouldn't know a Deep Purple B-side if it let down their tyres and tried to purchase a three-bedroom bungalow from them – but they couldn't appear to not know it. They were living out a new persona after all. So they just clapped and cheered.

It did the trick. We got our money and, with the exception of the lump on my head from head-butting a low-lying beam, we'd escaped unscathed. First show completed, and we only had another 27 to survive.

It was our first night of sleeping in the bus. Taffy drove a few miles down the motorway to Warwick Services. It was pretty much in between Leamington and Stow – the next evening's gig. We figured we'd park up, set the beds up, crack open a beer and listen to Pink Floyd until we passed out. It all seems very civilised, doesn't it? Well, it would have been if two knobhead coppers hadn't decided to get involved.

In fact, they weren't even real coppers; they were just a couple of jobsworths that were meant to be looking after the Services. It had obviously been a quiet night because these two were as bored as hell. They clambered onto the bus and were checking everything they could possibly check: the insurance, Taffy's driving licence, the MOT of the van ... You name it – they tested it. And failed, obviously, but they weren't giving up there. They spotted a crate of beer in the back. Thankfully, we hadn't touched that particular crate at this point.

"You're not allowed beers in a vehicle."

What kind of awful attempt at causing trouble was that? The rest of the lads didn't want any hassle, but Steve and I had had a few beers and weren't the greatest fans of authority at the best of times.

"What are you on about, mate?" I asked him.

"You're not allowed alcohol in this vehicle. We have a right to confiscate it."

Steve piped in: "They're not opened though."

"That's not the point. You can't have alcohol inside a vehicle – opened or not."

I'd had enough of him by that point. He had zero jurisdiction; he was talking crap. And I wanted a beer.

"Okay, mate, well that's bollocks for a start. So if I go Christmas shopping at an out-of-town Tesco, and buy my dad a bottle of wine, I can't drive it home, unopened in the boot of my car? You're talking shit."

The guy had no comeback. "Fine, well we'll be waiting by the gate and if you attempt to drive out in the morning with that alcohol, we'll be forced to confiscate it."

"Go for it, mate."

They drove off, we cracked open the beers, put on a bit of *Wish You Were Here* and drank to the opening night. The *You Have* tour had kicked off with a fair few "You have" moments.

Now this tour was 28 days long, and if I was going to tell you about everything that happened, we'd be here for a very, very long time. I assume you have a family that would miss you, so I'll just pick out a few of the events I think you'll find amusing.

The following night we were in a small village called Stow-on-the-Wold. It's a very wealthy Georgian market town about 45 minutes' drive from Leamington. Now normally, it wouldn't be top of the list of places for a punk rock band to play, but this quiet village had a pub called The Bell Inn. The Bell had a games room that was dedicated to John Entwistle, the bass player of The Who; and Stow-on-the-Wold was John's much-loved home town, so it's a fair bet that he'd enjoyed many a tipple in there. It had obviously become a massive haunt for rock stars and rock-star hunters. When I say "hunters", I mean people who are trying to meet their idols and maybe get stuff signed. I didn't mean some white South Africans with rifles, wanting to get Rod Stewart's head mounted on the wall of their billiard room.

John had been dead for a year by the time we played there. He died of a cocaine-induced heart-attack in a Las Vegas hotel room with a stripper/groupie at the Hard Rock Hotel and Casino on the eve of the band's US tour. Swap the cocaine for a bottle of Oban 14-year-old Scotch and you've got yourself the perfect death.

We arrived at the venue and it was as posh as hell. I'm talking far too posh for a rock 'n' roll band. There were two girls behind the bar. It turns out they were the two young girls that were sat on the giant speakers in that famous scene from Tommy, The Who musical. We'd basically just walked into a rock celebrity world, only with en suite rooms, four-poster beds and breakfast included.

We munched on some free food and then started to set up. I said to the girls, "Do you want us to play acoustic? It's quite smart in here and we are quite loud."

I was shot down in a blaze of laughter. "Have you not seen The Who pictures on the wall? We like our music rocking!"

We set up and then sat down with a couple of beers before we played. Then the customers arrived. You tend to get two types of audience – either the university crowd, which tends to be attractive young girls with borderline alcoholism and a gay best mate; or the middle-aged-man crowd of mid-life-crisis-driven accountants. The crowd at The Bell was almost entirely made up of lesbians. I'm not talking one or two; I'm talking 30- odd big, butch, crew-cut lesbians playing pool and skulling beers. I was actually quite intimidated. I think I was probably freaked out because I was in a roomful of women who had bigger balls than I did.

So, we start to play; get two minutes into our opening number and Taffy is sent outside to get the acoustic gear. I had foreseen that particular iceberg and I had warned them. "We like our music rocking!" Clearly not – and we'd started with a *ballad*!

The acoustic gear was quickly set up. I swapped my electric for an acoustic and Turlough played congas instead of a drum kit. That was all we changed and it did the trick. All was going great until a pint glass flew across the front of the stage. Apparently, the girls had had a disagreement as to whose turn it was to play pool. That's a normal reaction, I thought. I often throw pint glasses at people and start full-on 20-strong brawls over a game of pool.

During the whole gig there was this odd-looking middle-aged man at the bar. Later in the evening, the barmaid mentioned how cool it was to have a fan like him. I obviously asked: "Why, exactly?"

"Well, he follows you around the country in his caravan. He hasn't missed a show in two years. That's serious dedication."

We'd never seen this bloke before in our lives, and it turns out he didn't even own a caravan. But he'd told the staff some bizarre story about following us to the ends of the Earth.

There are some weird people about.

We finished our set and sat up at the bar having a few beers. Apart from the scrap, the gig had gone pretty well. We were two dates into our tour and both sets of audience had

liked what we'd done. That's all we hoped for, really. We were meant to be paid a couple of hundred quid and be given a couple of hotel rooms for the night. All was going well until one of the lads opened a tab on our gig payment. That's never a good idea! It ended up with us, a few of the calmer lesbians and a posh couple from down the road, all doing shots while Tim played Oasis songs from a "Learn Oasis" guitar book and the posh girl smacked the congas. It was all very odd.

Then the posh guy says, "I do a bit of MCing." I hate MCs and it's normally reserved for skinny cocaine-taking chavs with zero talent to rap (badly) about their "bitches and hoes". By "bitches" and "hoes" they're normally talking about the underage girl they knocked up that now lives with him in a single bed at his parents' house.

But this posh guy starts rapping. He was amazing! Honestly, he was really, really good! Plus, he was pretty witty and was tearing most of the spiky-haired lesbians to shreds. I think they'd have given him a damn good hiding if he hadn't been so good. I think you're allowed to insult people if you do it in a talented way. Credit where credit was due. Posh guy was pretty cool.

After another hour or so, I was about ready to die in a Las Vegas hotel room. Taffy was the same and we figured we'd head up to bed. The two of us left everyone else downstairs drinking our earnings. Now this was where the tour started to get odd. Taffy and I walked into our room and it can only be described as a honeymoon suite. So here I was, 22 years old, in only my boxer shorts, climbing into a four-poster bed with a Welshman in his 40s, also only in his pants. I always thought it might come down to me climbing into bed with an older man just to pay the rent one day. I had always assumed it would be with a married Conservative politician; and I wasn't even getting any money for this!

Taff flicked on the TV to divert our attention away from the obvious awkwardness, only to find a nice David Essex film for us to watch. I'll confess, it was quite romantic; and had Taffy been a beautiful woman, I could have gone for this. But instead we settled to avoid the spooning and both slept as near to the edge of the bed as possible.

When we got up the following morning, downstairs was pure carnage. Steve was nowhere to be seen. He hadn't stayed at the venue and he wasn't answering his phone. Taffy and I had one room and Tim and Turlough had the other. God knows where Steve had ended up. We started packing up the gear and I went to sort out the money. We owed them about £60! What the fuck?!?! Thank god the bar staff had had a good night because they wrote off the money we owed. While that was great, we still didn't have any money to chuck in the petrol kitty! We'd really have to curb this drinking a little bit.

We loaded up the van and there was Steve, passed out in the bus. "What the fuck happened to you last night?"

Steve looked very confused, and very cold.

"I'm not sure."

I spoke about this with him recently, and he still doesn't recall. See normally, you'd assume he must have met a girl and gone back with her. But Steve had something that no girl in that venue had wanted – a penis.

The following night was a Saturday. Fridays and Saturdays were the most important nights because they would normally have the biggest turnouts. I don't know if that's the same the world over; I assume it is. But in England we live for the weekend, and whatever takes your mind away from the mundane day-to-day nine-to-five routine.

We took a drive up to Peterborough. None of us had ever gigged in this town before so we didn't have a clue what to expect. We got lost again and again. It felt like a lifetime before we eventually rolled into this housing estate. Imagine the worst, most terrifying housing estate you've ever been to, and then multiply it. We were like lambs looking out from the sides of the truck as it pulled into the slaughterhouse.

"Taffy, tell me this isn't where we're playing!"

I'm making us out to sound like a bunch of pansies, aren't I? We are small-town boys, after all. And this place was a dive.

There were burned-out cars and boarded-up houses. Every street corner had another group of potential gang rapists stood on it. It was okay though – it wasn't like we were drawing attention to ourselves by driving up in a bright white bus with our website splattered down the side in massive lettering.

When we pulled up to the venue, our hearts sank even further. All that was missing was an Orange parade and flying petrol-bombs. It had every other ingredient you'd need to create a post-apocalyptic movie scene – smashed beer bottles, walls with articulate graffiti like "Shaz iz a phat slaaaag!" on them and fat, tattooed men smoking weed outside. Isn't weed meant to put you into a relaxed state? I dread to think what those guys where like when they were wound up.

I want to tell you the name of the pub. But at the same time, I quite like my kneecaps so I'll just call it "The Posh". Two reasons: one, Peterborough Football Club is nicknamed "The Posh", and two, it's the polar opposite of what the place was actually like.

I had the pleasure of booking this particular nightmare so I bit the bullet and walked into the pub.

"All right? Is the landlord about?"

Then a giant bloke, about seven-feet high and five-feet wide walked over.

"Who's asking?"

Umm, okay, well I'd just shit myself so that was awkward.

"We're the band. My name's Gareth. I spoke to you on the phone?"

"Oh, for fuck's sake!" he said, then just walked off.

That wasn't a reaction I'd ever received from a landlord before. I don't mean to sound like a snob and I've played some scary venues in my time. In fact, they're normally the best shows ... proper salt-of-the-earth people that appreciate what you're doing. But this place was different. It was genuinely scary and none of us really wanted to play there. Taffy was a double-hard bastard and had done years in the army, and even he wasn't comfortable with us playing this gig.

The landlord came back with a diary.

"I've fucked up, mate. I've double-booked you with a karaoke."

We were the most relieved band of all time. The landlord was genuinely sorry and was pretty gutted that he'd double-booked us. He was actually a really nice bloke and asked us if we wanted to stick around and have a few beers. We didn't. We made some excuse about having to head off to find a place to stay.

"Next time you're touring, book back here, mate. We'll have a good night."

"Will do, mate!"

We obviously had no intention of ever booking back there. We were straight back in the van and off on the road to Birmingham as quickly as possible. Not once in my life had I ever thought I'd be excited, relieved even, to be heading to Birmingham.

The day actually ended up pretty cool. We called at a corner shop and picked up a crate of beer and whacked the radio on. It was Saturday. Football day. In all the years before and since, this was the only time that all the results went our way.

Derby County 2 – Reading 1 meant I was happy.

Leeds United 3 – Coventry City 0 meant Steve was happy.

Liverpool 3 – West Brom 0 meant Tim was happy.

Portsmouth 3 – Crystal Palace 1 meant Turlough was happy.

Taffy hated football so didn't give a shit. Well, I say didn't give a shit. Until his local side Cardiff played and beat Derby he didn't give a shit. I had the pleasure of staying at his house in Wales a couple of years ago after a 6–1 drubbing. That was fun!

Anyway, I'm drifting off on tangents. Basically, never before had all our teams won on the same day. Small victories, I know, but when you've just been completely terrified by a housing estate that resembled a scene from a Vietnam-war film, you take what you can get.

I'll level with you, mate – there was no reason for me to tell you about the football stuff at all. It's just Derby don't win very often and I was kind of clinging to it for some comfort. I'll stop digressing from now on.

Right, I'll continue. We played all over the Midlands the next week or so. Birmingham was our main stop as we actually played three different shows in the city. Birmingham is the UK's second-largest city so you can get away with playing a few gigs in different areas. We'd have a few people follow us from show to show, but mainly it was a different audience at each venue. That was our perfect scenario. The whole point of us taking Kody on the road was to share our music with different people and build a fan base. On a personal level, it was pretty much to find ourselves. I know that sounds like the type of annoying thing you'd hear from a weird, tie-dye-wearing hippie, but it was true. We'd spent 90 per cent of our lives on a rock that was 26 miles long by 13 miles wide. We really needed to explore the bigger world, and drink shitloads of beer of course.

The gigs went pretty well, on the whole. Our drinking was getting a bit excessive and we weren't eating very well, but that was all part of it. We had been keeping a tab on the beers we drank. Whether it was a can of beer in the bus, or a pint in the pub, it was a notch on our personal beer post. I think I've already told you this, haven't I? Well anyway, if I have, I'm sorry. But after 28 days, mine was an average of 9.6 beers a day. Calculators at the ready. In fact, I've got one on my phone, hang on ... Okay, that's 9.6 multiplied by 28 days ... that's 278.4 beers in 28 days. I don't know what the .4 was. A Fosters, I assume. That doesn't count as a real beer. It's awful stuff; even Australians won't touch it.

We'd play our show and sometimes be given a place to sleep, but mainly Taffy would drive out of the city, find a service station and we'd park up for the night. Most service stations would charge £10 to sleep overnight and they'd have showers available in the morning. They were pretty grotty though. You'd walk in and find the pubic hair of a fat French truck-driver decorating the plug hole. Showering in service stations wasn't our finest hour. We probably came out dirtier than we went in.

If we turned up at one that was really bad, we'd just head back into the city to find a swimming pool. We'd get about five lengths in before our lungs started to collapse. I didn't mention that we all used to smoke back then, did I? Yeah, we were paragons of health and vitality! We'd delude ourselves that we'd sweat it out onstage and that we'd swim a few lengths every couple of days. But the reality was we went to swimming pools for the three S's: shit, shower and shave. The glamorous side of rock 'n' roll is definitely not sitting on a toilet with two bandmates either side of you, listening out for the plop. I'm sure Mick Jagger left that part out of his autobiography.

I think it was about two weeks into the tour and we were down in the West Country. We were playing a show at a place called The Phoenix, in Plymouth. We'd played there a couple of times before, and, while the venue itself was awesome, the surrounding area was a little bit dodgy.

If you don't know Plymouth, it's a town on the South West coast of England, and it's home to two things: the Royal Navy, and university students. That meant there were shedloads of bars, and shedloads of fights. The Navy lads would pile into the town after weeks or months of being trapped on a ship and they'd want two things: beer and sex. Or, if possible, a combination of the two. That meant that Plymouth was heaving with prostitutes, not least on Union Street. And where was The Phoenix? Yep, Union Street.

Like I said, the venue was great and the audiences there were always really cool. But they always arrived by taxi. Nobody was ever stupid enough to walk around Union Street, especially at night. Well, nobody except us.

We parked the bus outside the venue and cracked open a few beers. It was late- September but it was still pretty warm so we all sat on the roof of the bus skulling a few cans in the sunshine. You could see different girls working different corners, and it really did make you want to cry. I was 22, and in my eyes, now, that's still a kid. But these girls made me seem old. Most of them were around 16, and some of them looked even younger than that. Sleazy middle-aged blokes were regularly pulling up, picking up girls and then dropping them off a few minutes later. This went on for hours – literally a conveyer belt of people. One girl had more sexual partners in about 45 minutes than the whole band (Taffy aside) had had in our entire lifetimes. I don't actually know about Taffy's sexual past; he was just older so I assume he'd have brought the average up. I might get into trouble for saying that.

Taffy didn't seem fazed by any of this. The rest of us were gobsmacked and were caught staring and given the V-sign by various girls around the block. I asked him why it didn't bother him, and he just shrugged his shoulders and calmly told us that this was life for a lot of people. This was their reality and, in all the years he'd been around South Wales, he'd seen a lot worse than this. That terrified me. And it made me pretty angry at the same time. As naïve as it sounds now, I just wanted a million pounds so I could take all these girls away and save them. But, as Taffy said, a lot of them didn't want saving. That was the tragedy of it all.

One of the girls was slightly friendlier than the others. When I say friendly, I mean downright rude and obnoxious but not quite as horrible as the others. She was about 16 and she acted like many 16-year-olds do – pretentious and gobby. The difference was, unlike most 16-year-olds, she was pretentious and gobby in the brief periods of time between having sex for money with middle-aged men.

There was one young lad hanging around the whole time. He must have been about 18 and looked like a normal scruffy scallywag – the kind of lad you'd expect to see signing on, and then flogging nicked DVD players in the pub. We'd spotted him earlier and assumed he'd had his eye on our gear. But then this young girl came back, handed him

her money and went back to her corner. This kid was a *pimp*? He was barely old enough to tie his own shoelaces and he was pimping out girls? What the fuck is going on with our world? I really got the hump then.

The "friendly" girl came over and asked for a cigarette. Well, she didn't ask as much as demand one. Normally I meet rude with rude. If anyone else had spoken to me like that, I'd have told them to fuck off and that would have been that. But I'd seen what she was doing and the way her life had turned out. No doubt just a couple of years earlier she was a normal 14-year-old schoolgirl with all the dreams and aspirations of anyone else. But her life had been involved in a horrible pile-up and now here she was. *I'd* have been rude if the world had dealt me those cards. I gave her a cigarette.

As she reached out, I saw needle tracks on her arms. She saw the moment I spotted them and pulled her sleeves down. I gave her a sympathetic smile and for a split second her eyes softened, like she'd realised that we were all right. Then, when she knew she'd let her guard down, she put her stern face back on and walked back to her spot.

It was pretty obvious that her heroin addiction was the reason she was here. The nine- year-old pimp could obviously supply the drugs if she worked the streets. Where were her parents in all of this? It was truly heartbreaking.

The pimp was clearly pissed off that she'd come over to us and was glaring in our direction a lot. I'm blessed with something my friends and family affectionately call the "Icke Glare". This was put to full use and I was begging for the dickhead to bite. Now you need to know this about me – I'm not a violent man and I hate confrontation, but on this occasion I was bang up for it.

I was sat on top of the bus with a beer in my hand, going through different ways in which I could smash this lad's face into the kerb. That sounds a bit twisted, but if he was drowned in a bath no-one would miss him and so many people's lives would be improved.

I'd worked my glaring magic, and pimp boy had bottled the stare-out contest and turned away. Just as he had his back to us, the girl got into a red van. As the pimp turned back round and saw his girl had vanished, his face filled with panic. We were the only ones that had seen where she'd gone and what the vehicle looked like. What was the lad going to do? He needed to know where she was, but he also didn't want to talk to us. There were five of us; we were all pretty big and we'd made it perfectly clear that we thought he was scum.

He nervously paced over to us. I wasn't sure how this situation was going to pan out because I wasn't entirely sure of my own reaction. I wanted to just down the beer and put him through the window, but I also wanted to play a show that night.

"All right, boys? See where the blonde bird went?"

All right, boys?! Boys?! Who the fuck are *you*, mate?! *Boys?!* I'd have been less insulted if he'd called me a prick! But the idea of trying to be friendly and level with us like we were one and the same type of person – that just pissed us off. No-one answered him. We just stared at him. That must have been pretty unnerving for a guy that's used to intimidating others. He wasn't dealing with fragile young girls this time. Now he was on the receiving end, outnumbered and outsized by five blokes looking right into him. He looked like he was about to cry and call his mum and tell her some mean boys in the playground had robbed his dinner money. Just as it looked like the bottom lip was about to quiver, the red van pulled back up and dropped the girl off.

The pimp ushered her off and her shift was over. What a scumbag! I do think about that quite a lot actually. That was around six or seven years ago, so she'd be about 23 now – if she's still alive that is. Maybe she got her life sorted and is happy in a loving relationship. If I was a gambling man – which I'm not – I'd say she's still there. Which is sad.

Wow! That was uplifting, wasn't it? I'm not sure why I shared that. I've kind of brought the mood down. Does that jukebox have any Nick Drake? That would really finish us off, eh?

A couple of days later, we were playing over in Bournemouth. It's about another couple of hours back in the direction of the Isle of Wight. We used to play there quite a bit, as a lot of our mates had gone to university there. It was far enough away from home to make them feel like they'd made a break from the Island, but still only an hour and a half away from their mothers' home-cooked chilli.

I never had any desire whatsoever to go to university. It simply didn't interest me. I had moved out of the family home just before my 16th birthday so I'd done the whole living- on-beans-on-toast thing. Plus, as you can hear from these stories, I didn't really need to travel a hundred miles to discover a drinking culture. Sure, people do go to university to achieve things, but nine times out of ten they go to avoid getting a job for a few more years. I had a rock band. That was my way of avoiding getting a job – a "real" one anyway.

All that said, if I had wanted to go to university, it would probably have been Bournemouth. It was a big town that had all the stuff that cities have, but without a lot of the chaos that comes with city life. It has beautiful beaches and shitloads of bars. Shitloads of bars means shitloads of places for live music. We were sorted.

There was one venue in the town centre called "The Gander on the Green". We'd never played there before but had heard loads about it. When you get chatting with bands around the country, they'd always mention The Gander when they spoke about shows across the south coast.

Obviously, we were a fair bit pissed by the time we arrived. There is a theme appearing here. It was just a regular venue; just your usual pub. It had a bar, tables and chairs, and a stage. It didn't look anything out of the ordinary. I was a wee bit disappointed really. I don't know what I expected but I guess I thought something would have stood out. I wondered what all the fuss was about.

We set up the gear and played a belter of a show. A really awesome gig. It was probably one of our better performances of the whole tour. The difference it makes to have a decent sound engineer and a decent crowd. If you can hear yourself, that's a start! The amount of shows we played where, as a singer, I couldn't hear a single word I was singing. God knows what it must have sounded like; I dread to think. But this place was great. The sound was clear and people could actually hear the words. That was the most important thing for me. I put my heart and soul into the lyrics and it really used to piss me off when people couldn't hear them. Unfortunately, I was pissed off a lot back then.

I'm rambling. This gig was shit-hot, basically. There was a massive crowd and they were really into what we were doing. They'd never heard of us before but they'd come out with the mindset of having a good time and enjoying the bands. I wish more people were like that. But they really weren't. So many audiences used to stand, arms folded, with that whole "Impress me" attitude. That made the band uncomfortable. A hostile atmosphere makes it impossible to create a good show. These folks were different though.

After the gig, a few girls came over and invited us to a club. After a show like that we were all on a massive adrenaline high. Damn straight we wanted to go to a club! I had my all-nighter head on. If I was asleep by the time the sun came up, I'd failed.

We really didn't know Bournemouth all that well so the girls hopped in the bus and started directing Taffy as to where this all-night session was going to kick off. Once on the road, we decided to play a little game. It's pretty odd but was always a good laugh when we had a bus full of strangers. It was called the "Yes/No Game", and there was only ever one player.

First, let me explain. Our drummer, Turlough, lost his virginity at 12 to a girl the same age at school. Very young, I know, but perfect for the Yes/No Game. Tim would be the question master and Turlough would be in the hot seat.

"Yes/No Game, Turlough."

"Oh, for fuck's sake."

"Now, we just want yes or no answers. We don't want you to explain anything. Just yes, or no."

"This is getting boring."

The girls were pretty intrigued by all this. I think they thought they were going to get some juicy gossip from the road. They got more than they bargained for.

"Okay, is your name Turlough?"

"Yep."

"Are you a leopard?"

"Nope."

"Do you live on the Isle of Wight?"

Sigh. "Yep."

"Do you drive a tractor?"

"No."

I was already laughing by this point because I knew where it was going. The girls obviously had no idea. And remember, Turlough was a six-foot-tall fourteen-stone bloke with a beard. It just made the next question appear worse.

"Have you ever inserted your penis into a 12-year-old girl?"

There was a giant pause.

"Yes or no, Turlough?"

Turlough exhaled, looked at our new passengers and replied.

"Yes, but I was ..."

Tim interrupted, "Just yes or no is enough."

At that point, we reached our destination. I've never seen a group of girls in high heels move that quickly before. I got the feeling we wouldn't be seeing them again for the rest of the evening. It didn't matter. We all had girlfriends and it was worth it to see the look on their faces. How to lose fans and alienate your band. That should have been the name of our album.

The club wasn't a club at all. It was just a local pub that had painted its walls black, whacked some neon beer-lights up and got a late-night licence. Not that any of us cared. It had a bar and punk rock music. I was in nirvana.

After a few whiskys, the beer-drenched dance floor became more appealing. I was attempting my usual breakdancing moves. They tend to come out when I've had a few too many. Obviously I can't breakdance in any way whatsoever. But that was all part of the fun. Or so I thought anyway.

Apparently, the owner wasn't a fan of my particular moves. Okay, so I'd occasionally barge into the odd Goth accidentally; but that's not such a bad thing, is it? They're all desperately in need of a sense of humour anyway. I thought I was doing my best to bring down the suicide rate in the county of Dorset. If the weird lad cracked a smile, maybe his very pale girlfriend would do the same and they'd both stop hating their parents. It was unlikely, but worth a try.

According to Taffy, the owner-guy was tired of giving me warnings and had gone off out to the back in a huff. I don't remember ever getting a warning. I vaguely remember grabbing him and trying to get him to dance with me, but that's about it.

The owner was a big chap with long, bleached-blond hair. He was probably about 45 and figured the greys wouldn't show up so badly with blonde hair. He was dressed completely in black, with combat trousers and a T-shirt that I'm sure fitted quite well 10 years earlier. I think he was going for that hard-nut biker look. That doesn't work for me. Whenever I see a guy dressed head-to-toe in black, I think of stagehands at a West End musical. Which I'm guessing wasn't the image he was going for. I'm not sure what that says about me. Two years of studying drama, I suppose.

I got so much stick for doing drama at school. I was one of only two lads in a massive class of girls. I used to get called "gay" by the sports bunch. Hang on? You do PE with a load of lads. You get changed, showered and do physical activities together. I get physical contact with attractive girls; I get changed in the same room as them and so I get to see them in their underwear; plus, I get to act out passionate scenes with them for four hours a week. And *I'm* the gay one? I was always confused by that.

Why have I told you about my drama classes? I'm not the best storyteller, am I? Sorry.

So yeah, mid-life-crisis guy wasn't a fan of me. That's fine, I thought. I wasn't thinking of inviting him on a 10-day tour of the Greek Islands so it really didn't bother me if he liked me or not. That was until he came back out with an iron bar.

I may have taken the goading just one step too far this time.

Taffy was doing his usual sober panic and trying to get us lads out of the place as quickly as possible. We were all far too drunk to be in control of ourselves. In fact, drink or no drink, none of us were fit to be left in control of a video game, let alone our own lives.

I kept telling Taff that it was fine and that everything would be cool. They'd starting doing an alternative karaoke by this point. There was no way I was missing that. I'd managed, with my dance moves, to win back a couple of the girls from earlier. I had obviously informed them that Turlough was 12 years old himself at the time of the aforementioned sexual encounter. Once they realised we weren't trying to fill the paedophile band-slot that had just been vacated by Gary Glitter, we were okay again.

I went over to the karaoke guy and signed Tim, the girls and myself up to sing Iris by the Goo Goo Dolls. Everyone loves that song. We'd be safe singing that one.

Various weird-looking people were getting up on stage and massacring classic songs. That's the whole point though, right? Surely no-one goes to karaoke to listen to good singers? I want my songs out of key. I want wrong lyrics and, if possible, I quite like a few tears when the girl realises she can't actually "do a great Belinda Carlisle". I'm a bastard like that. I only watch ice skating on TV in the hope that they'll fall over. I should probably prepare myself for eternal damnation, huh?

Taffy and Tim were chatting to the landlord and he was starting to come around. He still had the metal bar at the ready but he hated me slightly less now. He even asked Tim what I was taking as he wanted some.

"He's not on anything. That's just how he is."

"Oh."

The karaoke guy announced: "Tim and Gareth singing Iris by The Goo Goo Dolls. Come up to the stage."

There was a bit of a roar as the dancing had made us mini-celebs in the bar. Plus, like I said, everyone loves that song.

Tim was less enthusiastic.

"What are you doing, Gareth? I don't know that song."

"Of course you do. Everyone can sing that song."

"You sing it on your own then."

"I don't know it well enough."

The guy kept calling us up again and again and the crowd of people was getting quite annoyed. The landlord came over.

"Is that you again?!" he shouted at me.

"I'm off."

I bolted for the door, quickly followed by the rest of the band, Taffy and the two girls we'd managed to win back over. We all bundled in to the van and Taffy stepped on it.

"Where the hell are we going?" asked Taff.

"Anywhere away from here, mate", was the overwhelming response.

I'd pretty much walked into a guy's pub and made it my mission, unconsciously of course, to make his evening a complete misery. I think if he'd got hold of me, I'd have woken up in Bournemouth General Hospital.

In the end, we drove back to the girls' house. They shared a place, and it had somewhere to park. We could leave the bus there for the night and actually get a warm night's sleep. We'd been in the bus for the last few nights so a simple living room floor was like a five- star hotel to us.

When we arrived, one of the girls was really worried about us making a mess. It was a rented house and the landlord was a bit of a nightmare, apparently. We assured her that we were all adults and that we wouldn't trash the place. And normally that would have been the case. But on this occasion, they had a dartboard. None of us are particularly good at darts at the best of times, let alone after a skinful.

I threw the first dart, missed the board and made a hole in the wall. "Oh, fuck."

We rearranged a few pictures and the room looked as good as new. It looked nothing like their living room used to look and it was pretty obvious that they'd notice eventually. We just hoped that because they were also a bit drunk, they wouldn't notice until they had sobered up. By that point, we'd be off on the road to the next show. It worked.

We all sat around drinking tea, and neither of them noticed. It really wasn't subtle either. There was a picture where even the most Feng-Shui-obsessed hippie wouldn't have even considered putting one. But in true Kody style, we blagged it and got the hell out of there in the morning.

A year or so later, we played a show and they turned up. I was bricking it. But they said nothing. They must have assumed that someone else had done it at a party or something. They'll never know though, eh? I mean it's not like I'd go around admitting it or anything.

A few of the shows we played on the tour were real last-minute piss-in-the-wind bookings. We knew that the gig probably wasn't going to be that great, but if it filled an evening and we got to play to a few new people it would be worth it. One of these gigs was in Walsall. Walsall is basically just a part of Birmingham, although that would probably offend the locals a fair bit. None of us had ever been there and none of us ever really felt a desire to go there. But, like I said, a gig is a gig and we had made a pact to play anywhere and everywhere.

When we used to pull into any new town or city, the plan was simple. "Taffy! Find a puuuuub!" Taffy would find us a Wetherspoon pub and we'd be set up for the day. J D Wetherspoon is a chain of bars that stretches the length of Britain. I'm normally a fan of the local, less-sterile boozer, but with "Spoons" we'd get clean toilets, cheap beer and food, and plenty of well-hidden plug sockets that we could charge our phones without anyone noticing.

Taffy found a parking space in the centre of town and we all piled out to find a Wetherspoon. Bear in mind, it was no later than about 11 am and the first thing we saw was a pissed-up bloke fall off a bench backwards and knock himself unconscious.

"Welcome to Walsall, lads."

I was starting to dread the evening's show because it was one I'd booked, so any misfortunes that lay before us would feel like my responsibility. I hadn't got a great vibe from the landlord on the phone so my optimism was non-existent.

I figured the best option was just to get plastered and make the best of the night. We found a Wetherspoon in an old converted theatre, and got straight on the beer. Another good thing about that particular chain of boozers is you rarely, if ever, get any trouble in them. During the day they tend to be full of old alcoholic men that just sit and chat about "the good old days". Well, Walsall wasn't like everywhere else. We'd probably only had a couple of pints each and we'd already seen a couple of blokes ushered out with blood pissing out of their noses. God help us this evening, that's all I could say.

The pub we were playing was called The Dog & Partridge, the same as this imaginary place. And, incidentally, it wasn't too dissimilar to this pub I've described either. We walked in and immediately felt uncomfortable. I think the landlord took one look at us and regretted booking us. We were only playing acoustically, but the way we dressed and carried ourselves made us look loud. Does that make any sense? We didn't look like a bunch of lads that was going to make sweet background music that the locals' conversations could drown out. And, if that was what they were hoping for then they were right to be concerned.

We were going to play two 45-minute sets with a 15-minute break in the middle. The deal was that we'd be sorted out with a few beers and they'd have a whip-round at the end to try to get us some petrol money. Obviously it was a crap agreement, but it was a free evening and if we weren't playing we'd only be sat in a pub spending our own money.

The first few songs were met with complete silence. The pub had a few people in it but not one of them gave a shit that we were there. We had a song called *I Once Swallowed Lego*, and I thought that since no-one was listening I'd get away with joking that it was about me being abused as a child and that "lego" was in fact a euphemism for something else. Well, that was the only time the people decided to listen. Not to self: jokes about child abuse do not go down well in Walsall.

So here we were, playing to a bunch of people that couldn't stand us and now hated me personally for my slightly warped sense of humour. We were just about to play our last
song of the first set and all I could think about was that we had another 45 bloody minutes of this crap. Then Tim went into an incredible speech.

"Listen, everyone. We're just going to play one more song and then we're going to have a little break. I just wanted to say thanks a lot for taking the time to listen to us. We love touring and playing to salt-of-the-earth, honest, hardworking people like yourselves. Our problem is that we've just signed a massive major deal with Universal, and as of next month we're not allowed to do this anymore. We just wanted to come out on the road one last time and play to fantastic people like you. As of next month it will all be television appearances and posh venues. So thanks a lot for allowing us here to play one last time."

The entire speech was bollocks and completely made up. Turlough was laughing, but managed to hide behind his congas. I, on the other hand, was centre stage and had to hide my laughter by bowing my head and pretending that I was genuinely upset by not being able to "slum it" anymore. Steve and Taffy both looked completely confused.

We finished our last song of the set and put down our guitars so we could chill out for 15 minutes and have a beer before getting back up there to drag ourselves through another 45 minutes.

All of a sudden, the landlord piled out with trays of food. They'd laid on an entire buffet of samosas, sausage rolls and sandwiches – the works. The locals were all surrounding us, buying CDs and T-shirts. Absolutely insane! They'd hated us 10 minutes ago, but because they now thought we were about to become famous they jumped on the bandwagon.

For the whole of the second set, they were up dancing and loving every minute of it. What's funny is that although Tim had lied and said we were going to be superstars or whatever, the songs hadn't got any better. We were still the same band that they'd hated earlier! People are strange creatures, aren't they? Grub was nice, though.

A couple of days later, we ended up heading up north towards Manchester. In those days, we slept wherever we could. Basically, Taffy would drive until his eyes were struggling to stay open. Once we'd nearly crashed a couple of times, we knew it was time to stop. It didn't matter where it was. The van would pull up, sleeping bags were rolled out, and bang, we'd be dead to the world.

On this trip to Manchester, Taffy had got shattered around Rochdale. I think it was only an hour or so from our destination but there is no point carrying on when you're struggling. So we parked up in some back street next to a factory. We figured that we'd be up and off to Manchester well before anyone from the factory appeared.

Taffy parked up, and the rest of us hit the pub for a few late beers before bed. Obviously, a few beers turned into a gallon or two and we were all pretty hammered. We all got in the bus and passed out. Well, all except for me and Turlough. We stayed up most of the night texting Taffy's phone, because his text alert was so annoying. It was Yoda from Star Wars. "Message from the dark side there is." It was very irritating, but we found it hilarious. The next day, Taffy was very confused as to why he had 28 blank messages and a tonne of missed calls. Apparently, you can't wake up a Welshman.

Talking of not waking up, that's where the story gets funny. I was woken up by banging on the side of the bus. We all gradually rose and peered out of the window. Taffy opened the door and there stood a very young, very panicked-looking police officer. Behind him was a group of equally panicked-looking factory workers.

"Hello?" coughed Taffy, while losing that first wedge of morning smokers' mucus.

"Oh, thank God you're alive!"

"Eh?!"

The policeman was visibly relieved and the factory workers had all broken into smiles. We were all very confused.

I piped up, "What's going on, Officer?"

Turns out we'd overslept. The factory staff had come in to start their morning shift and had seen the bus. After glancing through the windows and seeing our lifeless bodies, they'd phoned the police reporting a mass suicide. No wonder the copper looked so confused when he saw us all looking out of the window at him.

I laughed at the time but, thinking about it, how offensive is that?! A large group of people had looked at us and said, "Yeah, they're dead". Do I look that bad when I sleep?! I suppose I must.

We did make up a news story while we were driving on to Manchester. Because Taffy was older, we used to wind him up about his age. Tim was explaining how the national press would have reported our suicide, had it happened.

"Four men in their twenties were found dead in Rochdale with what appeared to be a prehistoric caveman's body lying amongst them."

Taffy didn't laugh.

Okay, so the tour went on a fair bit and by the end we were all struggling. The diet and the booze hadn't helped of course, but, most of all, we just wanted to go home for a few days. Touring is great, don't get me wrong. But this was our first attempt, and like most first attempts it had its negative moments. We were all skint and the gig money was barely keeping the bus in fuel. It wasn't really keeping us in fuel, y'know? We needed some decent food that had been cooked in something other than a deep-fat fryer.

Steve had gone to Tesco and stocked up on shedloads of tinned food – stuff you could eat cold like beans, tuna, rice pudding and tinned fruit. It made sense because it was a

much cheaper way of doing it. Plus, his food would actually have some goodness in it. The rest of us all grabbed a sandwich and a pot of pasta or whatever – a more expensive way of doing it, but an easier way.

We piled up the motorway towards Coalville. It's in North West Leicestershire, so a fair drive from our shows down south. We were tucking into our grub in the bus. Steve wouldn't stop going on about how little he'd paid for his big stash of tins. He kept saying that we were mugs for paying over the odds for plain-tasting sandwiches when his stuff would keep him going for days. And, to be fair, he was right. We were penniless really, and should have been more careful with the cash we were spending. But what Steve hadn't done, much to the amusement of the rest of us, was buy a tin opener.

"Hahahahahahahahahahahahahaha!!!!!"

I don't think the load of us had ever actually laughed that hard before. We were now speeding down a motorway, miles from anywhere. A starving Steve had a huge stash of food that he couldn't get into. We shouldn't have laughed really but given the huge speech about how we were mugs, it would have been rude not to.

Steve was pretty pissed off now, and did what Steve did when he was pissed off. He went to sleep. Honestly, that guy could sleep for hours and hours. It was bizarre. I mean, I am a man that actually struggles to sleep. Even if I'm at home, I'm on sleeping pills a lot of the time just to get a few hours. But Steve could just pop his head on a pillow and he'd be off in dreamland. I was jealous as hell of that. Every single member of that band snored, and so I was almost always tired. I'd end up lying awake, feeling like I was in a scene from *Planet of the Apes*.

Turlough once woke up to find me in complete meltdown. It was about 4 am and I'd got zero sleep because of the snoring. He found me in a foetal position, punching myself in the head, screaming, "I can't do this anymore!" Sleep deprivation does terrible things to a person.

Anyway, sleep deprivation wasn't something Steve had to worry about. He caught enough winks to turn a lesbian straight. Maybe that's where he'd disappeared to back in Stow-on-the-Wold?

Steve slept for the whole of the journey. We got to Coalville and found a cheap boozer for a couple of beers. We left Steve in the van. Once he was gone, there was no waking him.

Coalville is what the name suggests – it's an old coal-mining town. All the pits had long been closed and I have no idea what the local economy was funded on. Drinking, I think. There was a hell of a lot of pubs for a place so small. It actually reminded us of our home town in that respect.

After a couple of drinks, we made our way up to the bar we were playing. It was called "The Vic Bikers Pub" and it looked scary! What's amusing is years later we played several shows at the venue and found everyone to be amazing. They were real nice, friendly, honest people. But in that split second, we judged. We saw massive motorbikes and massive blokes riding them, and we shit ourselves.

I think we sold ourselves short in those days. The truth was, we could mix it up with all the big boys and we could hold our own against any metal or punk bands. But we always saw ourselves as small-town boys that were far too feminine to stand up and play to these kinds of people. It simply wasn't true, and we should have played that night. But we didn't.

"Vics" is an old mock-Tudor pub that used to be simply called "The Victoria". The guy had bought it and turned it into a rock venue that catered mainly to bikers. We were supposed to be opening for a couple of local metal bands that evening. When we walked in, we thought we were going to get eaten alive. The leather-clad locals seemed to have a strange look in their eyes. It was like they were choosing which one of us would go better with chips and onion rings. In hindsight, they were simply looking at us like any local does to an outsider. They were just wondering who we were. It was nothing sinister. And, like I said, we went there loads in the years after and had some amazing nights. But that night, we didn't fancy it.

It was probably the lack of sleep. Maybe it was the horrible diet, or, more likely, the booze. But we were all paranoid and thought it best if we made an excuse and got the hell out. We weren't getting paid and I'd only managed to blag us on the bill, so they wouldn't care and we weren't letting anyone down.

We grabbed a couple of beers and had a huddled chat at the bar. Steve was still asleep in the van. He would be our perfect excuse. We'd simply tell the promoter that our bass player had eaten some dodgy fish and had food poisoning. There was no way we could play without him so unfortunately we'd have to pull out. Problem solved.

We all went over to the promoter. Like all promoters you need to give bad news to, he was massive. Why can't they be average height, average build – you know? Nope, they're always built like a wrestler and covered in tattoos of skulls and knives. We had the pleasure of having to tell him our predicament.

But who wouldn't believe us? I mean, we'd got here. It wasn't like we just weren't going to turn up. But the guy wouldn't have it. He kept asking what he'd eaten, where he'd got it from and what his symptoms were. It turns out the bloke had contracted food poisoning from eating some fish a couple of weeks ago. Why the hell did we have to pick *fish*?! We could have gone for any other meat. But no, we had to choose what the promoter had just had.

"Where is he?"

"He's asleep in the bus."

Then, the promoter stomped outside towards the van. What the fuck were we going to do?! If he woke Steve up, that would blow the whole story. Steve hadn't been briefed on our plan. He had just been asleep the whole time. We chased the guy out into the car park. The guy clambered onto the bus to find Steve sparked out across two sets of seats. He had his head buried under the blanket and literally looked like a dead body.

The fellah started to shake Steve's corpse.

"Don't wake him, mate. He needs his rest."

We tried to pretend we were concerned about our bass player. We were more concerned about our kneecaps.

Steve starting to stir, and his confused face peered from beneath the blanket.

"Jesus Christ!" said the promoter. "When you said he was ill, I though it was just a stomach bug. This guy's got it a lot worse than I had."

Steve's face was completely puzzled. But thank God he was so confused that he said nothing. The guy was talking Steve through what he needed to do – what he needed to get from the chemist and everything. I'll be honest, this was too much for me. I had to leave the bus because on the inside I was shitting myself laughing. I was trying so hard not to let it spill out into the open.

Tim held it together really well and was even taking notes about what medication Steve would require.

"Just cancel the rest of the tour, lads. Look at him! There is no way he's fit enough to play any more shows."

We thanked the promoter-guy and said that we'd park up somewhere and then head back to the Isle of Wight in the morning.

Taffy drove out of the car park and back onto the main road out of Coalville.

"Right," said Steve. "Is anyone going to tell me what the fuck just happened?"

5: A MONSTER'S STAPLE DIET

Poole, Dorset, 2004

Band members:
Gareth Icke – Vocals/Guitar
Tim Pritchard – Guitar
Turlough Ducie – Drums
Ollie Ducie – Bass
Taffy – Roadie/Driver

Back in 2003 and 2004, all we did was tour. We would all pile into the bus and hammer it to anywhere and everywhere. We weren't fussy about where we played. We just desired two things: beer and an audience. As long as people were listening, we were happy. In our minds, the first couple of years were for paying dues – working hard and getting the crap shows out of the way so we could feel like we'd earned any success that might come our way. I'm sure that sounds weird as most people would just focus their eyes on the prize. We, on the other hand, were focused on the idea that if we got the prize, we'd earned it.

By the end, we had a booking agent and they would take care of booking up our tours. But back then, we were still doing it ourselves. Our rules for booking tours were simple. When we played a show, it would fall into one of three categories: The good gigs would go into the "definitely rebooking" pile; the shit gigs would go into the "definitely *not* rebooking" pile; and then there was the grey area of pile three. If the gig was shit, but something about either the venue or the promoter showed promise, we'd book it one more time and then slide it in to pile one or pile two, depending on that show's outcome.

The Central Bars in Poole was a 100 per cent category-one venue. From the outside it was just a regular Victorian-looking pub. It didn't really look like a music venue at all. In fact, it looked just like The Queen Vic from the TV soap, *Eastenders*. Perhaps that's what they designed it around? It had really high ceilings, giant mirrors on the walls and a huge wooden bar that ran the length of the room. If you dressed the locals up in flat caps and tweed jackets, you'd think you'd accidentally stepped into a time machine.

When you got upstairs it was totally different. The walls were painted black and covered in old punk rock posters. Old tour flyers from the likes of Led Zeppelin and Black Sabbath littered the place. At one end of the room was a small bar, and at the other a nice big stage. It was simple, and that's the way we liked it. Dark and dingy venues were always perfect for making a racket.

We'd played here a couple of times and always had an absolute blast. We'd always managed to blag the perfect slot – middle band of three, between two local acts. As a supporting band it meant you rarely got paid, but it did mean you were guaranteed an audience. See, that's the problem with being an out-of-town band – no-one knew or cared who you were. They were there to see their mate's band, not ours. But by being on second, it meant that you got the fans of the first band and the fans of the third band to watch you. And most of the time we'd win a fair few of them over. I feel I have to confess this too: Normally we were straight-down-the-line honest blokes; but occasionally we'd tell the odd white lie. If we were playing with a couple of bands that were pretty poor but had a big following, we'd gush about how great they were on stage.

"Before we start, can I just get another round of applause for the opening band? I'm sure we'll see them on MTV in no time."

That's pretty sad, isn't it? But sometimes you have to do what you have to do to get people onside. That's the sad thing about music at that level – it's often seen as a competition. In our eyes it wasn't, because we were happy doing our stuff and letting other bands get on with doing theirs. But often with young bands, they'd bring along their mums, dads, brothers, sisters, aunties and uncles. Hell, some bands would even wheel out grandma for a swift brandy. When we walked on stage after their beloved son or daughter, we'd often be greeted with crossed arms and a hostile attitude. We would be in a no-win situation with them. If we played really well and blew their kid's band off the stage, they'd hate us. And if we got trashed and performed badly, they'd hate the fact that we were higher up the bill than their kid. So that's where the false compliments came in. There isn't a parent on the planet that doesn't enjoy hearing how good their child is. It's underhand, but it often worked.

So, we'd done that supporting gig a couple of times and then the landlord invited us back for a headline show later in the year. That's always worrying because, like I said, we were an out-of-town band and, therefore, it's hard to be sure that you'll get people in. The landlord wasn't having it though. He said he'd book us for Halloween and get two local bands to support us and promote the hell out of the show. We figured that Halloween nights are always busy and, with the two local acts, we'd be pretty safe on the audience front. So, the date was written in the diary and we added a few dates around it along the south coast.

I think we were playing in Exeter the night before Halloween. We used to play there a lot, so the law of averages would suggest we did. For the benefit of the story, let's pretend we were playing in Exeter. It's only about an hour's drive from there to Poole so we arrived at The Central Bars pretty early on the day of the show.

Some shows you panic about and some you don't. All the anxieties would be the same with new venues. Will there be a decent crowd? Will we get paid? Will the soundman be a dick? None of these were an issue at The Central Bars as we knew it was a decent place and we knew the landlord was a cool bloke. No panic needed here – just a nice relaxing drive along the coast. That was until we arrived.

Taffy parked the bus around the back of the pub and we went to walk in. It must have been around lunchtime and our plan was to say a quick hello, whack our gear up in the venue and go to get some food.

"Lads," I said, "there isn't one poster up anywhere."

Normally, the outside of The Central Bars was covered in posters and they really went to town on the advertising. This wasn't boding well, but maybe the two support bands he had were so well-supported that they didn't need to advertise. I know that's clutching at straws but we did that a lot.

Once we got inside, we asked the barmaid to tell the landlord we were here and we all took a seat at the bar.

The pub looked completely different. It had gone from the beautiful and immaculate Victorian boozer we all remembered, to the inside of Satan's holiday home. I've never really been one to celebrate Halloween but they went all-out with it here. There wasn't one painting or ornament that wasn't covered in some kind of fake cobweb or neon glowing witch. There were literally ghouls and ghosts in every nook and cranny.

The landlord appeared at the bar, stopped in his tracks and stared at us all. He looked like he'd seen a ghost that wasn't of the decorative kind, and although the dead are meant to rise on Halloween I was pretty sure we weren't actually dead yet.

The guy's name was Adam, and he was the youngest landlord I'd ever met. I think he was only about 25 or so. He was really skinny and about a hundred feet tall. I don't know what it was with us lot and stupidly tall people. We seemed to attract them.

Adam was stood there, frozen to the spot holding a three-foot, bright-green skeleton. "There's been a monster fuck-up."

Well, I was gone completely. We were all in fits of laughter. Of all the terms Adam could have used on Halloween while holding a plastic skeleton, he had to say the words "monster fuck-up".

It turns out that with all the hassle of running the pub, Adam had completely forgotten about the show. He hadn't booked any support bands, got a sound engineer or advertised the show at all. Indeed, that was a monster fuck-up.

The guy felt so bad but, at the end of the day, these things happen. Everyone makes mistakes and it was hardly a big deal really. We'd played on the south west coast the previous night and we were off to play in Southampton the following evening. We'd have had to drive through Poole anyway so no harm done. Adam said we were more than welcome to stay at the pub and get involved in their Halloween fancy-dress party. He also said that he'd keep us in beers all night. That was all the music any of us needed to hear. Free Snakebites all night? Fuck Halloween – this was Christmas come early!

The five of us ordered beers and set about spending the rest of the afternoon propping up the bar. I love local pubs purely for the clientele. You really do get some interesting characters coming in and out of the doors. And Adam knew each and every one of them.

You'd hear the door squeak as it opened and you'd judge the customer by Adam's reaction. Most of the time it was just a regular nod and a polite, "Hello, Jeff", but occasionally his eyes would roll and the "Hello" would be preceded by a muffled, "Oh, for fuck's sake" under his breath.

One such "for fuck's sake" reaction was to a heavy-set bloke with no legs, in a wheelchair. He was wheeled in by his mate and then lifted onto his regular bar stool. The whole pub went quiet, and people were completely engrossed with this guy. I mean it's not everyday you see a bloke with no legs get hoisted up onto a bar stool; but I'm not a fan of staring and it made us feel a little uncomfortable for him.

"Pint of cider, please, Adam," said the man.

"I can't serve you, mate," replied Adam.

Surely this wasn't because he was an amputee? The fellah was sober and so I didn't see a reason why serving him a drink would be a major inconvenience.

"You can't serve me? Why the hell not?!"

Adam took a deep breath and exhaled.

"Look, mate ... You've just lost both your legs because you've drank so much cider over the years. I can't morally stand here and serve you a pint of cider when you've just got out of the hospital."

He had a point, to be fair, and I was kind of with Adam on that one. If the bloke wanted to drink himself to death in a public park then that was his prerogative; but this was Adam's pub and he would have to accept a certain amount of responsibility if the guy became ill as a result of drinking in his establishment.

The guy gestured for Adam to come closer and moved his body forward so they were just a couple of yards apart (I would have said that they were a couple of feet apart but it seemed like too much of an obvious joke).

Anyway, the fellah looks Adam in the eye and says, "So you won't serve me because cider has caused me to lose my legs?"

"Yeah."

"Well, maybe you could explain to me just how the fuck I'm going to lose any more legs from drinking cider?"

Adam looked over at us lads and smiled. "Fair point." And then he started to poor the man a pint of scrumpy.

Just like that, the pub went back to being rowdy again and everyone continued their conversations.

Like most conversations in a bar, it quickly turned to football. It's a common ground with men in English pubs. No matter what walk of life or ethnic background, you can always find safe middle ground with football. So the five of us and a couple of local fellahs got into a giant debate about the state of the game and the amount of money involved. You know the kind of conversation?

"Footballers are just overpaid prima donnas."

"Yeah, let them work one day down the mines and then we'll see what kind of men they are."

I don't entirely agree with that, and if there is that much money in football then I'd rather the players were getting it than the suit-wearing businessmen upstairs in the boardroom. But the truth is, there shouldn't be that much money in any sport and it's the common supporter that is picking up the tab. So, I explained my opinion and stated that the working-class man is forever being financially raped in this day and age. It probably wasn't the nicest term to use as a description but it was just a throwaway line in a conversation about football.

Then, from nowhere a female voice piped up: "I was raped once." Once again, the bar fell silent.

Shit, I thought. I'd opened a can of worms here. I really should choose my words more carefully:

"The working-class man is forever being financially *crippled* in this day and age"? Nope, I couldn't have said "crippled" either because of the cider guy. Maybe I should just

have opted to say nothing?

Anyway, I gulped and looked at Tim thinking I was about to get an ear-bashing off a slightly scary, alcohol-weathered, middle-aged woman.

Out the blue came, "Oh shut up, love," directed at the woman.

Some bloke at the end of the bar who had remained silent for the entire time had just piped up. The guy had just sat there with a pint, and when he needed it refilling would just get eye contact with Adam, and nod. He hadn't said a single word to anyone. But here he was telling the woman to shut up. She just sat back down and the pub went back to being noisy again.

I'd love to one day have the power to cause an "O.K. Corral" moment in a pub. I just hope I don't have to lose my legs or get shot by anyone to achieve it.

The five of us drank up and headed into town to try to find some stuff to dress up in for Halloween. As it happens, we passed another pub showing the football scores and ended up getting sucked in there. My team, Derby, was once again beaten. We lost a lot back then. Mind you, we still lose a lot of games now. But back then we were millions in debt and on the brink of going bust. Being a Derby fan was a painful experience. It certainly didn't help on the drinking front, and our costume-shopping mission was replaced by drowning sorrows.

So back we stumbled to The Central Bars. We were all slightly drunk, and without costumes. But now I had the added bonus of being put in a bad mood by my football team.

In the end, I think all we did was nick a barmaid's eyeliner and draw some stitches and stuff on our faces. We were the worst-dressed people at the party, but by the end we were also the drunkest and loudest. That made up for our lack of ambition on the costume front.

Adam had said he was going to keep us in beers but I don't think he had any idea just how much the five of us could polish off. I'm sure we'd nailed at least 10 or 11 pints of Snakebite each before we even got started on the top shelf.

Tim came staggering over with his video camera. "So what did you think of the Derby result today, mate?"

Derby had lost 2–1 to Queens Park Rangers and Tim was only bringing this up to try to get a laugh out of people. He succeeded, and a few of the locals were taking great pleasure in mocking me and my club of choice.

"What do I think of it, Tim? Honestly?"

"Yeah," slurred Tim. "Tell everyone at home how it made you feel to once again get beaten by lowly opposition."

I leaned over the bar and the first thing I saw was an industrial-sized staple gun. The bar staff had used it to put up some of the bigger, heavier wall decorations. I grabbed the staple gun and, as the whole bar stopped and gasped, I planted two staples straight into my forehead.

The place fell silent and I slammed the gun back down on the bar. Tim just stood gobsmacked, pointing the camera directly at my face. I could feel the blood slowly running down from my forehead and onto my face.

"That's how it makes me feel," I said, before swinging back round and necking what was left of my pint.

I guess that was my "O.K. Corral" moment. And at first it didn't hurt, but as I ripped the two staples out of my head I realised that they were quite nicely embedded in my skull. That's when the headache kicked in and the blood began to pour. There are only two cures for a headache like that: sex or booze. I resigned myself to the fact that I'd be sharing a sleeping bag with Turlough that night and so perhaps I should take the booze option. So, with a bar towel held to my head, Turlough and I got the whisky flowing.

After a while, we realised that Taffy and Ollie had disappeared. Tim and I went back to the bus to see if they'd gone back to pass out. When I climbed on board, Taffy was fast asleep surrounded by foil trays and half-eaten Chinese takeaways. There was no sign of Ollie, so Tim and I got stuck into to the leftover food. A few minutes later, Ollie clambered onto the bus.

"You okay, mate? Where you been?" I asked him.

"Didn't really want to have a wank in the bus with Taffy asleep, so I had one out in the car park."

Now that seems like a bizarre conversation to be having, but in those days it was regular. My response was simply, "Oh, okay," and then I went back to the Chinese.

Tim, Ollie and I sat chatting in the bus for a bit as Taffy lay there, asleep. Normally at this point we would have got a pen and started work on decorating Taffy's face. You couldn't fall asleep first in those days without fear of getting drawn on. But on this occasion, Taffy's face was already covered in fake stitches and spider webs and stuff so we simply left him to sleep.

Then, from nowhere, a figure bolted past the bus in the darkness.

"What the fuck was that?" I asked.

"I'm sure that was Turlough!" replied Ollie.

What the fuck was Turlough doing legging it out of the pub, past the bus and off up the road? Then another figure flew past the window of the bus.

"Okay. That was a fucking witch!" I shouted.

It was about 2 am on Halloween and were all battered. But even in that drunken state, we wondered why the hell our drummer was being chased up the road by a witch!

And when I say witch, I'm not being mean. I'm saying a woman dressed completely head-to-toe as a witch. She had the big pointy hat and was holding a plastic broomstick under her arm.

About 10 minutes later, Turlough appeared back at the door of the bus. He was completely out of breath and all he could muster was, "Lost her", before collapsing down into his seat. It turns out that one of the bar staff had taken a shine to Turlough and had attempted to kiss him. It just so happens that her costume was that of a witch and Turlough had been freaked and thought it best to run. Why he didn't just say, "No thanks" is beyond me. Come to think about it, what girl chases a bloke up the road for a kiss?!

God knows what Adam must have thought of us that night. Our bass player had a wank in his pub car park, our drummer had lost him one of his staff out in the streets of Poole in the middle of the night, and I had one of his blood-stained bar towels wrapped round my now-scarred head.

We all started laughing at Turlough as he was still gasping for breath.

"Turl?" I asked. "Do you think John Bonham was ever chased down the road by a witch?" "Probably."

Band 5 Piece - With Dan Hill in our brief spell as a five piece.

Band NY - In Chelsea Hostel, New York. I look like a tourist.

Brecon Beacons - Relaxing in the Sun with no idea what was about to happen.

Bus nudity - Turlough being Turlough.
No caption required.

Fancy dress - A normal night out in
The Solent Inn.
Note the drunken scar on my forehead.

Clean cut manager - Me in London in my clean cut period with manager Mike Sheath.

Klub K - The launch night of the 1981 single. When things really looked positive.

G Sleep - Asleep while drunkenly texting.

Kody Marquee Club - Live at the Marquee Club in Leicester Square.

London Photoshoot - 1981 promo
shoot in Central London.

Ollie Oar - Gig in London in which
Ollie arrived clutching an oar.

Loughborough - Rocking out in Loughborough on a UK tour.

Ollie NY - Ollie recreating the pose that got us in trouble on a flight to New York.

Outside half moon - The Kody Bus outside the Half Moon in Putney.

Steve Squadron - Steve in the Royal Squadron, where it all began.

(Above) Taffy Bus - Taffy assessing the damage after a high speed collision.

(Right) Taffy NY - Taffy learning the hard way not to fall asleep.

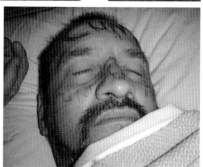

Tim theatre - Tim at Ryde Theatre, Isle of Wight.

Turl Exeter - Turlough at the Cavern in Exeter. I have no explanation for this.

Turl G - Me and Turlough being, well, mates.

(Above) Turl Tim - Turlough and Tim. "Find a pub!"

(Left) Waking up in the bus - Me and Turlough in the Kody bus.

(Below) Waterrats - Live at the Water Rats in Kings Cross.

6: GETTING SMASHED UNDER THE ARCHES

The Cavern, Liverpool, 2005

Band members:
Gareth Icke - Vocals/Guitar
Tim Pritchard - Guitar
Turlough Ducie - Drums
Tom Ladds - Bass
Taffy - Roadie/Driver

We were off on one of our many tours. By this point, they had all kind of merged into one another. Sure, there were always one or two stupid events that would stand out, but normally we wouldn't remember where and when. It was more a case of, "You remember when we woke up in that bloke's shed?"

"Vaguely."

This tour was different though because we were playing The Cavern in Liverpool – the home of the Beatles! Now, as much as we liked to be seen as a punk rock band, we all loved the Beatles. When asked who we thought the best band of all time was, it was a no-brainer. I'd already say, "The ..." before the question was finished.

We had a couple of dates booked across the South beforehand; then we'd play the Cavern, followed by a one-off date all the way up in Newcastle. It would mean a fair bit of driving and very little pay, as venues like the Cavern don't pay you. But it was all worth it just to say we'd played there. Plus, Channel 5 was coming to film the show. Channel 5 obviously isn't the biggest TV station in the world, but it's still a national TV network – and who were we to be picky? It was a great opportunity to get our music heard across Britain.

The first few dates went pretty well. I can't even remember where they were, to be honest, but they went okay anyway. We just saw them as warm-up shows. We'd try out a few different sets and see what went down well and what didn't. That would give us some idea of what we should do when we got to the Big One.

On the morning of the show, we arrived in Liverpool, parked up, and headed in to have a look around. We'd played in the city a few times, but it was always a quick dart-in-and- dart-back-out-again kind of affair. This time we'd decided that we'd get there early and

actually have some time to chill out first. I don't know why we were taking that side of it so seriously; it wasn't as if we were preparing to take on Germany in the World Cup final.

Tim is a massive Liverpool Football Club fan. And, despite being born on the Isle of Wight, he was walking around the city like it was a mighty homecoming. This was the place he was meant to be born, with the club's red livery running through his veins. Instead, he'd been born to a prison guard and a nurse in Newport on the Isle of Wight. I personally think he lucked out by not being born in Liverpool, but then I'm a Derby fan – I would say that.

The rest of us were trying to enjoy walking around the city but couldn't help but feel a certain tension in the air. I don't know if something was going on that we weren't aware of, but it felt like it could kick off at any moment. If Taffy had flipped his Zippo to light his cigarette, it would almost certainly have lit the blue touch-paper and lead to the death of thousands worldwide. Okay, so maybe that was an exaggeration. But it was a very odd sensation indeed.

Liverpool was named the European City of Culture the following year. I wonder if a city of culture is required to have at least three "Greggs" bakeries every ten yards. If that's the case, Liverpool was as cultured as they come.

After watching a couple of punch-ups between local toothless alcoholics, we made our way back to the Cavern. It's in an old part of town where all the streets are narrow and cobbled. And to be fair, despite my previous verbal battering of the place, I could see culture here. This part of town I could get behind. It's the kind of area that isn't affected by time. It had the look of the 1950s and early 1960s, with beautifully restored terraced buildings.

We literally felt like the Beatles must have felt way back then. We believed in what we were doing enough to think that we just needed one chance to make it. A break that would allow us to show the masses what we could do. And who knew, it might even be this night. It happened for them; it could happen for us.

I've never been a fan of the term "following in the footsteps of ..." I always thought people should make their own paths in life. But if we had to follow in someone's footsteps, who better than the greatest band of all time?

We moved the van so it was just outside the venue and we chucked our gear downstairs. The Cavern is literally that – a cavern. It's situated in the arches underneath the terraces of red-brick buildings. Tim and I had guitar stacks that weighed an absolute tonne, and so the 70 steps down to the arches was a fair old trek. Mind you, nothing gives you inspiration and energy like seeing your name on the venue wall. The bricks of the walls were covered in names of the bands that had graced that stage – the biggest in the world and the who's who of music. And there we were, right up there with them. Okay, we

didn't have our own brick, but one day ... Who knew? Tonight it could be a tatty poster, but next year a permanent lump of terracotta. Anything was possible in our minds.

I wish I still thought like that. But age, and knockback after knockback, kind of beats that out of you. Hopefully, there is still enough in the tank to stop me from becoming a bitter old man.

Right, we'd lugged the gear downstairs and cleared off for a beer across the road. It was the Champions League final between Arsenal and Barcelona, and where better to watch it than in Lennon's Bar. I have a confession to make: I was cheering on Barcelona – the only bugger in the whole pub to do so as well. In my defence, this was a time when Arsenal was diluting the Premiership with a sea of foreign players. They were probably less English than Barcelona. At least Barca has an English flag on its badge.

Enough about football but to say Barcelona won and I got glared at a lot; but worst of all we'd broken our no-beer policy. We were actually going to play this one sober. I know that's not very rock 'n' roll, but with Channel 5 coming to film it we figured we should at least be a little bit on the ball. But you can't *not* have a few beers while watching football, can you? Or maybe we were just all borderline alcoholics? Perhaps.

Even Tom, our new bass player, was in on the act. He was so innocent when he first joined us. When he first signed up in the Solent Inn, I think he actually ordered a pint of Fosters (4% Australian lager; or as I like to affectionately call it, "cat piss"). That was quickly banned and he was on the "1664" with us. And I wonder why so many things went wrong over the years?

The lot of us went back down to the Cavern and got on with the show. We were on pretty early, but that was to be expected. We were an out-of-town band and needed local acts above us to try to draw in the crowds. They did a pretty good job and, as far as Channel 5 was concerned, it was a pretty good show.

There are two reactions to having a camera shoved in your face: you either shy away from it, or you embrace it. Well, this was our big moment and the load of us practically shagged the hell out of it. The audience lapped it up and we were on fire.

Take the cameras out of the equation and take away the audience. The most important thing for us was where we were. Kody was at the Cavern in Liverpool! And not just that, but we were making that stage our own. We didn't feel or look out of place in a venue with that amount of history and reputation.

Do you remember before when I said that if we got to a certain time of the day and shit hadn't hit the fan, we'd start to get concerned? Well yeah, it was like 11 pm and apart from a couple of Scousers knocking the shit out of each other, nothing that could constitute a fan-hitting had yet occurred. That was never a good sign. See, I was a big fan of said shit flying _early_ in the day. It usually meant that we were safe for the evening. Like, a few years earlier we'd played an important show at the Wedgewood Rooms in

Portsmouth. While I was walking towards the venue in broad daylight with my sister and my girlfriend, some bloke just smacked me on the shoulder. My sister hit the roof and chased him down the road. But I was fine, because I knew it meant the show would go well. And indeed it did. But as I said, nothing had gone wrong yet.

Taffy ran upstairs to get the van opened up while we did a post-gig TV interview. How good does that sound? I'd purposely avoided wearing a grey T-shirt. The colour grey and sweat don't go too well together and no-one wants to see a sweaty bloke on TV. Well, unless you're a housewife watching Jonny Depp, while your real husband looks more like Jonny Vegas. But yeah, generally, sweat stains are to be avoided. Instead I opted for a pastel green T-shirt. Yeah, Gareth, real smart, mate. Exactly the same result.

Taffy came flying back down the stairs halfway through the interview. He looked like he had just been chased from his log cabin by an axe murderer.

"You okay, mate?"

"The ... v... va ..."

"The what?"

Taffy hadn't run downstairs so fast since he was in the army. There had been a fair few cigarettes, fry-ups and lagers since then. He was fighting for his breath.

"The van has been smashed."

"What the fuck?!"

The interview was abandoned and we all flew up the stairs. There was our poor van, battered and bruised and emptied of most of its contents. Thugs had smashed the door's window in with bricks which they then left discarded next to the bus. They had taken the stereo, the satellite navigation system, a digital camera and a few other bits and bobs. Thank God we were playing at the time and had all our musical equipment with us.

Whoever had broken in had obviously been disturbed because they had left a fair bit of stuff. We were touring, so all our clothes and trainers were in the back. So that's great, they were disturbed enough to do a runner and leave us with at least a few of our possessions.

It gets better though. On the windscreen was a sticker that said "POLICE AWARE". So, hang on, the police have attended the scene and stuck a sticker on the van saying they're aware, and then they've cleared off?! So now the van is left wide open for anyone else to help themselves to whatever the original thieves failed to claim!

Now, I'm no detective, but if I saw a van with "www.kody.co.uk" painted on the side and parked outside a world famous music venue with posters saying "KODY" on the walls,

I'd take a punt that the owners of the van were inside said venue. Then – and remember I'm no Columbo – I'd have walked into the venue and said, "Who is Kody? Only their bus has been broken into." And we'd have come outside and prevented any more gear being nicked. That just seems like common sense to me. Or am I wrong?

So there was our shit-hitting-the-fan moment. Sleeping in the bus is fine when the windows are all intact, but without them it's pretty chilly. And not only that, but without the sat nav how the fuck were we meant to find our way to the next venue?

An amazing day had just gone from hero to zero in about thirty seconds. There was shattered glass everywhere – all over our stuff and inside our sleeping bags and blankets. Liverpool had never been particularly high on my places-to-visit list but it had now fallen right off the bottom.

The door window was about the height of a regular bloke and about the width of a fat bloke, so six foot by four foot – a pretty big window to replace in terms of cost, and a pretty damn big hole to have to drive with. Driving out of Liverpool felt like we were strapped on the wing of a jet plane, only with shitloads of paper and wrappers flying around our heads. We really should have tidied up more often!

That night was up there with some of the coldest experienced in the Kody bus. Luckily, it wasn't winter. Had it been, we'd have died – simple as that. We'd come close to that in the past actually. Once, in Redditch, near Birmingham, it was so cold in the bus that I even texted my ex-girlfriend to tell her that I loved her and that I would always be there to take care of her, no matter what. I know that sounds melodramatic, but it was literally that bad. We were all blue and breathing clouds of our breath into the air. It was so bad that in the morning the venue fed us hot bacon sandwiches through the window of the kitchen and into the window of the bus. Once it reached our mouths, it was already ice cold. Dark days, they were. Mind you, what doesn't kill you and all that. Although it was probably our self-esteem that took a bigger knock than anything else. Unless you've tried to wee out of the door in temperatures like that, you've never felt like a woman. It was so cold that I needed a microscope to locate my penis.

So yeah, the big "we're going to be the Beatles" plan went out of the broken window. That is unless Lennon & Co. had had to blag a Plexiglas window from some rogue garage in Birkenhead. If they ever had to do that, then yeah, we were fully filling their bootprints. I think Birkenhead is where Cilla Black is from. That explains a lot.

Tim's dad, Dave, sorted out paying for the window for us. Thank Christ for that! We'd have been royally screwed without it. There was no way that we could have got to Newcastle, and certainly no way we could have got all the way down to the Isle of Wight, in that state.

But nothing else could go wrong, right? I mean, we only had to get to Newcastle, play a show and then go home again. That's easy enough.

We arrived in Newcastle. Phew! That bit was done. The new window had lasted the journey. I don't want to judge people but the two fellahs that fitted it looked like "Bodge It & Leg It".

We were playing at a little bar near the River Tyne. It would only be an acoustic set, but after the hassle of the previous 24 hours we were up for a chilled-out evening with no great events.

We unloaded our gear although we weren't needed for a couple of hours. The five of us went for a walk and quickly located the two vital ingredients for any decent afternoon: an off-licence and a football pitch. We grabbed some beers and made our way to the park. There is nothing like nailing 30-yard passes while spraying beer all over yourself. Tiny pleasures, I know. But in those days, I'd just broken into the England Beach Soccer team so I took my football pretty seriously.

I looked up and saw Turlough running long. I curled a perfectly weighted pass into his chest before hitting the deck in a crumpled mess. There was a snap and an intense pain that I can only describe as like being shot in the knee. What's sad is I even looked around, half expecting to find a sniper peering out of the bushes. What the fuck was that about?

The lads helped me up and I hobbled to the side of the pitch.

"You okay?"

"It's nothing. It'll wear off."

I drank through the pain as all men in their twenties do. But Christ, did it hurt. That was another reason to be relieved that that night's show was a sit-down acoustic set.

The show went pretty well. We sold a few records and got a good reception from the locals. All I could think about was drinking through this agony. I'm not that bad normally, and my pain threshold is pretty high by all standards. But this smarted horribly.

Once the gear was loaded, I skulled a beer and set up a bed. If I was asleep, I wasn't in pain. I never believed in painkillers. This is a belief that I've since walked away from. Now, I practically live on them.

I was out like a light, and the next thing I remember is waking up with the sun shining brightly on my face. That wasn't right. We should have been on a boat way before the sun was shining that brightly.

"Taff, where are we?"

"On the motorway, mate. Engine's blown."

"You are fucking kidding?!"

So much for nothing else going wrong. We were just outside Winchester, only an hour from home, awaiting the AA to arrive with a recovery vehicle. This shit only happened to us. I mean, sure, everyone breaks down – but not that often!

'I got up and fell straight back down. "Aaaaaaaagggggghhhhh!!! FUCK!"

I'd forgotten about my knee.

The lads were all sat on the hard shoulder and Tim was playing acoustic. I grabbed a couple of bottles of cider and hobbled outside. It was only about 7 am, but we'd had enough shit and deserved a drink. Plus, I needed something to numb the pain.

By the time the AA guy arrived, we were a fair bit tipsy and singing songs by the roadside. It got us a few beeps from passers-by, so we treated that as our applause.

Vrroooom!!! Beeep!!!! Vroooom!!

"Thank you. Thank you!"

A tour that had started so well had ended in farce. Mind you, we should have been used to that really. We started off full of hope and enthusiasm and we ended up drunk on the side of the M3.

Oh, and apparently kicking a ball to Turlough can tear your knee ligaments. Who knew?

7: BREW YORK, BREW YORK

New York City, United States, 2005

Band members:
Gareth Icke - Vocals/Guitar
Tim Pritchard - Guitar
Turlough Ducie - Drums
Ollie Ducie - Bass
Taffy - Roadie/Driver

This story is less about music and more about living the rock star dream (obviously, without actually being a rock star). But then, I suppose a lot of *being* a rock star is a state of mind anyway. How many times do you reckon I can use the term "rock star" in one minute? That's four already.

Anyway, it was April 2005 and we'd basically been touring solidly for about six months. As soon as we'd got home from the *You Have* tour the previous September, we were set up with management and re-located to London. Then, from the capital, we were sent out on tour all over the place. It was amazing, obviously, and it was the whole reason we were in a rock band. But at the same time, six months of playing shows and recording and writing all took its toll. We were emotionally and physically drained and needed a break.

We weren't your average live band. When we performed, we performed. It was always pretty energetic, and so after that many shows our bodies were starting to show signs of wear.

Plus, in March we were in a recording studio completing our debut album. We had 15 days booked in a top studio in East Sussex. Now most bands would attempt about four tracks in that time – if they rushed. We had to record and mix 15 songs in 15 days. That's pretty much impossible. And yet we managed it. But only by putting in 12-

hour days and not taking breaks. Needless to say, by the time the two weeks were up, our already worn bodies were in a state of collapse.

The record was sent off to be mastered and we were given two weeks off to recharge ourselves before we'd have to tour again.

Tim's 21st birthday was at the beginning of April, and his folks paid for us all to go to New York for a week. What an incredible gift! I'm pretty sure his older brother, Ben, had been bought a car for his 21st and so Tim's folks said he could have a gift of equal cost. Tim decided to take me, Turlough, Ollie, Taffy and his older brother, Ben, with him to the Big Apple.

Have I mentioned Ben before? I think I may have as he used to tag along a fair bit and he helped us out loads with web design. None of us are technical in the slightest so Ben was our clever website man.

Ben's a good-looking, fashion-conscious fellah about a year older than me. I think he owns about a hundred pairs of trainers, and he will colour-coordinate them with whatever T-shirt he's wearing. I'm sure that takes a lot of planning, but he always looked good so I guess it was worth it. The rest of us were always too lazy for all that. I'd often just throw my clothes on the bed and get Ben to pick me an outfit. He was like our very own Gok Wan, only not oriental and ever-so-slightly less camp.

So, the six of us were off to "the city that never sleeps". I'm not sure how advisable that was for a bunch of lads that were in desperate need of a relaxing break.

I have always had a huge obsession with New York for as long as I can remember. I have no idea where it came from, but the city always excited me. When I was an ice hockey player, I'd always be dressed head-to-toe in New York Rangers' gear. I'd stay up all night drinking coffee as a teenager, just so I could watch the Rangers live on TV. Yet despite my obsession with the city, I'd never been. This trip was as much a pilgrimage for me as anything else – a rite of passage in life or something. Okay, maybe that's a bit dramatic. It was six drunken buffoons going for a week-long piss-up. But "pilgrimage" sounds more civilised.

We were flying with Virgin Atlantic. In those days, Virgin was the number-one airline in the world. It was seriously flash, and, for a while anyway, we felt like we'd landed. No pun intended, of course. Okay, maybe a little bit of that pun was intentional. Just humour me. Long-haul flights also mean one thing: free booze.

The six of us were scattered in twos across the aeroplane. I was sat next to Ollie, and after a couple of hours we were seriously on the beers. I'm not the greatest flyer so I always need a couple to calm me down. But that's when I'm flying easyJet and they're charging £3 for a half-sized can. I could only afford a couple in that case. But these were free, and we were on holiday.

Ollie and I had the most volatile relationship of the band in those days, so I think we both figured that a holiday in New York would be a great way to hang out and build a bond between us. That could only benefit the band, too.

Another hour or so later and we were pretty wasted. Ollie had found these packets in the chair in front that contained luminous-green eye patches, travel socks and a

toothbrush. Now, I don't know what possessed us to do this but, well, yeah I do know what possessed us. It was beer, obviously, but anyway ... the pair of us put these bright- green socks over each of our ears, put the blindfolds on and started dancing around the aisle. Normally the passengers would have a good laugh at two idiots, and maybe we'd just get told to sit down. But what we hadn't noticed was that this plane was full of orthodox Jews. They all had the side curls that – apart from the colour – looked a lot like our sock-ears. But Ollie and I were blindfolded and had no idea that all these folks had taken offence and were slowly getting out of their seats to confront us.

After a little while, we took off our blindfolds and our fits of drunken giggles were met with a sea of religious blokes with their stern faces on. The pair of us removed our "ears" and sat back down. Oops! Maybe we should just watch a film or something.

I seem to have the knack of unintentionally offending Jewish people on aeroplanes. Years later, I was flying to Tel Aviv to play football and our coach was watching Borat on his laptop, with the volume up. It seems that laughing hysterically while a man sings: "Throw the Jew down the well ..." is frowned upon on a flight to Israel.

I don't know if they do it anymore, but Virgin used to have this text-messaging service where you could type in a seat number and it would send a message to that person. I guess it was so that people who had been separated could keep in contact throughout the flight. I found it hilarious! When I got up to go to the toilet, I'd make a mental note of select people's seat numbers. If I spotted a sleazy-looking bloke who was obviously away on business, I'd send him a message saying I was a young woman up for some fun and did he fancy meeting me in the bathroom.

"I saw you in the queue and I thought ... he looks like he has a VIP ticket to the Mile-High Club."

See, I think that's funny. But when the guy is frantically looking around in a state of semi-arousal, and then I give him a cheeky wink and a wave, the amusement seemed to bypass him. His loss. I thought it was hilarious. I doubt Virgin still has that text- messaging thing actually. Ollie and I surely can't have been the only ones to horribly exploit it. I'd be offended if we were.

In New York, we were staying at the Chelsea Hostel in Manhattan. Not the world famous Chelsea Hotel, but just around the corner. The difference that one letter can make ...

When we arrived it was pretty late, but Ben and I were in US-time now. We hadn't come all the way to NY to go to bed; we wanted to get on it. Everyone else was pretty much ready to hit the sack so Ben and I figured we'd leave them to it. Ben had been to the city before and knew his way around the bars. Taffy, on the other hand, wasn't having any of it.

"Nope. You're not going out without me!"

"But, Taff, you look knackered, mate. We'll be fine."

He wasn't having it, so he joined us for "protection". A fat load of good he did. What our evening consisted of was me and Ben grabbing a beer, chatting to locals and having a laugh while Taffy was slumped asleep at the table. We'd stick stuff on his head and get the barman in for the obligatory thumbs-up-next-to-Taffy shot. Then we'd wake him up and move on to the next bar.

Ben and I continued this for about three hours all across Greenwich Village. Goodness knows what they thought of us – two slightly drunk young Englishmen dragging around a sober and exhausted, tattoo-covered, 45-year-old Welshman.

Once we got back to the hostel, we were ushered into our sleeping pits. The rooms each had six beds, which would have been perfect if one of the rooms would have been empty so that we could bunk up together. Turlough, Ollie and I ended up in one room with another three blokes; and Tim, Ben and Taffy went in another.

In our room, there was a silent Irish lad who looked like he'd snap if the wind was too strong. He was travelling the world with his girlfriend who had ended up in a different part of the hostel (something I found very odd). He was a nice enough kid but didn't really say anything and looked intimidated most of the time. Then there was a rude Australian who we couldn't be bothered with and really doesn't require a description. And then there was Barry.

We didn't see Barry until the morning as he'd stumbled in while we were asleep. He was about five-foot-eight, quite stocky and had a shaved head. He was a doorman back in Kent, England, but he'd decided one day to just piss off around the world. Barry looked like a doorman. In saying that, basically, he looked like a hard nut. But after a minute's conversation in the morning, we all decided he was the funniest bloke we'd met and he was now member number seven of our group.

The seven of us found an empty six-man room and moved our stuff in, and set about hitting New York hard.

If I asked you to describe a hostel, you'd describe this one. Pretty old and bare but with all you need to sleep. The place wasn't designed to be lived in. But then why would you go to New York to hang out in a hostel anyway? Our plan was to sleep there and explore the city the rest of the time. We'd got quite lucky with our new room though, because a) we were all in together so we could lock it up and not have to panic about our stuff getting nicked, and b) our room was on the ground floor and opened straight out onto the courtyard. It was a small area but it had benches and stuff so people could sit out and have a few beers in the evening. It was pretty cool, and I don't know whether it was because we were a rock band or because we had a double-hard-looking Barry with us, but everyone gravitated to us in that hostel. After a couple of hours of being around the courtyard, we'd inherited an Australian bloke, his sister and two Icelandic girls called

Passion and Valdis. Our six-man holiday was turning into an eleven-person bid for New York domination.

To be honest, every day of the trip was pretty much the same. We'd all wake up hungover, Taffy would grab us all Coke, then we'd go and do tourist stuff during the day. We did all the cliché stuff: Empire State Building, Madison Square Garden, Ground Zero – all the stuff that you have to see to say you've been to New York. Then we'd head back to the hostel with a load of beers and sit outside in the courtyard before it was time to go out and hit the town. We did have a great time during the days doing the tourist stuff, but it was really all about the nights. I'll just tell you a couple of stories that I reckon you'll find amusing.

On one of our first nights there, the six of us, plus Barry, Passion and Valdis, went out into an area called Bleaker. It was only a couple of subway stops from us but it was at the heart of everything cool. Bleaker was a whole massive street of bars, all playing live music until crazy o'clock at night.

This particular night, I don't even think we'd gone out with the express intention of getting battered. It was more like a few quiet beers, enjoy some live music and then chill out at the hostel. Nights like that never go to plan. We walked into this bar and there was a guy sat in the corner playing Jane's Addiction on an acoustic. It sounded awesome. There is a lot of crap out there but this lad could play. Plus we're all secretly fans of Jane's Addiction so it worked for us.

Tim walked up to the bar and ordered two pitchers of Budweiser. The barman says: "You want to flip a coin?" "Eh?" "Heads you pay, tails I pay."

Tim obviously agreed and it came up tails. The barman just said, "Cheers", slid over the beers and went off to serve someone else. So we stood there having just won eight pints of beer because of the flip of a coin. I think at that point we all knew that the "quiet few beers" plan was going out of the window.

We kept going up and buying more, and every time we'd flip a coin. Some we lost and some we won. But either way, we were still getting free beers about 50 per cent of the time. Obviously the barman wanted our custom and banked on still turning a profit, but it was working out pretty well for us and we'd have only spent more money elsewhere.

You know how it is when you've had a few beers. You always get the taste for more. We all had our clubbing heads on now. Let's find a decent club and drink away until the sun comes up. We had just one condition. We needed to find a club near the hostel so we didn't have to stagger far on the way back. And the two Icelandic girls had one condition too – they wanted to go to a gay club. That sounds like a bizarre request for two straight
women but it did make sense. Both Passion and Valdis were absolutely stunning. Like, magazine-cover stunning. They were both petite, with Passion being brunette and Valdis being blonde. It was pretty much most blokes' threesome fantasy all in one little Icelandic bundle. If ever they went into "normal" clubs they'd get hassled by blokes, so they preferred gay bars where they wouldn't get any guys

touching them up. That was fine by us. We just wanted to drink – it didn't matter where. Plus, deep down, I reckon we quite liked the idea of getting some attention ourselves for once. Wherever we'd gone with the girls, they stole the limelight. At least in a gay club we'd be the party piece.

There was a club just around the corner from where we were staying. It was called "Rawhide" and it had a loose cowboy theme. I'm sorry, but that's the best name for a gay club ever! Plus it had "Men's" and "Men's" toilets. I loved the place!

By the time the male dancers came out, we were all pretty wasted. This one bloke came out in just a thong. I actually coughed out most of my drink when he appeared. He had the biggest cock I'd ever seen in my entire life. I haven't actually seen that many, to be fair, but it was pretty impressive nonetheless. Passion's eyes started to water. Then in a sweet accent she said, "That will just hurt, no?" I agreed that perhaps a girl of her size was not suited to a man of his.

Tim and I ended up posing for photos while putting money in his thong. Tim had to take it one step further and actually squeeze the thing. His reasoning was that he needed to make sure it was real. It was. While I was posing for pictures, I genuinely thought the thing was going to break loose from its thong and attack me. I mean, I'm pretty tall but because he was on a podium the penis was at about my chest height. The last time I'd had anything even vaguely similar to that near me was at the zoo. And even then it was mildly sedated.

Turlough was at the point of drunkenness where he genuinely didn't know where or who he was. He was leaning up against a wall in the corner, with an untouched beer in his hand doing that dribble bubble thing that drunks do.

"Turlough, mate, you going to get involved? Give the dancer some money!"

We were expecting Turl to stumble over, pop a dollar in the guy's thong and pose for a photo. But no, Turl was way too pissed for that. He just reached into his pocket, grabbed whatever coins he had and threw them at the podium. Everybody ducked, but the big- cocked dancer took a body full of shrapnel. Everyone kicked off and the dancer guy went mental. Turlough just stood there swaying. He genuinely didn't have a clue what was happening.

I flew over and grabbed him and ushered him out of the door. We were all trying to pretend we were angry with him and that he'd let everyone down. The truth is, on the inside, I was absolutely crying with laughter. That was such a Turlough thing to do. He was trying to be nice and yet it backfired completely. We apologised on his behalf and

the dancer seemed to calm down – which was lucky because the club was full of beefed- up guys and I didn't fancy brawling with them, especially since the toughest one of us was Turlough and he was in no state to be fighting anyone.

The beautiful thing about friendship is that you're there for one another in each other's time of need. Another beautiful thing is that you know each other's weaknesses and so know when best to strike at someone's vulnerability. The next morning, Turlough was vulnerable and we were prepared to strike.

"Really let yourself down last night, mate." "Why, what happened?"

"I just never had you down as a homophobic, mate. It's really disappointing. I thought you were a better man than that."

"What?!"

Turl had no recollection of the night before, so remembered nothing of the money- tossing incident. Obviously we told him about it, and we exaggerated. We told him that he'd been goading the dancer and calling him a "faggot" before throwing coins at him. None of that was true but Turl didn't know that. We kept it going on and on all day, and even Barry and the girls joined in. They were all very disappointed in who Turlough had turned out to be.

I know we were mean but because we knew Turl was the least homophobic person in the world, we knew we could exploit his desire to prove his innocence. And boy, did we do that. Basically, we made Turl believe that the only way he could prove he wasn't homophobic was by going back into Rawhide that night and kissing as many gay men as he could. So, armed with a Polaroid camera, that's exactly what we did. I can't remember how many middle-aged blokes he got in with that night, but it was a fair few. And each and every incident was captured beautifully on film.

"Well done, mate – you've proved you're not anti-gay. We're all proud of you."

I'd love to say that that was the end of it, but it really wasn't. See, that's the trouble with capturing moments on film – they have a nasty habit of backfiring later on.

When we got back to the Isle of Wight, we'd all gone to our local – The Solent. Ben had brought down this huge pile of Polaroids to show everyone. Most of them were just drunken smiles, as well as a few shots from the top of the Empire State Building and stuff like that. My personal favourite was one of me in a subway station with my arms around two police officers in front of a sign saying that anyone taking photos on the subway would have their camera destroyed. Apparently, these two coppers weren't briefed on this new anti-terror law because they were both giving the camera a big smile.

But anyway, in among the pile were the pictures of Turlough and his many male conquests. The pictures had been handed around and everyone had all had a good laugh. Once everyone had had a look, I put them on the bar and we went back to having some beers. Soon after, Turlough's then-girlfriend walked in. Now no-one even thought about the pile of Polaroids and what might happen if she got hold of them. You know where this is going, don't you? I was in the middle of an in-depth conversation with Ben so neither of us was concentrating on anything outside of each other's words. Then, out of the corner of my eye I saw her reach for the photos.

"Are these the pictures from New York? I haven't seen these yet."

Oh, no! Everyone just looked at each other in frozen panic. What could we do? We couldn't exactly snatch them out of her hands, could we? Well, I tried anyway. I think I said there were some dodgy naked pictures of me in there and that she shouldn't really look. I said I'd sort them out and then she could see them. The plan was to rip out the ones of Turlough and the kissing and pretend they were pictures of me. But she just raised her eyebrows and said:

"It's not like everyone hasn't seen that already." Damn me and my drunken nudity.

We all saw the moment she got to the photos. First the mouth went wide open, then the look of murderous terror as she flicked through the Polaroids faster and faster. I grabbed my coat. I think I heard as much as a "What the fu ..." before I was out of the door and on my way home. There was no way I was sticking around in that war zone.

Oddly enough, their relationship didn't last too long after that. Mind you, neither did her friendship with us all. I think Turlough's excuse of "Gareth and Tim made me do it" might have put a nail in that particular coffin.

Right, back to New York City. Every story seems to take me back to the Solent Inn. I reckon that place might be at the root of most of my psychological problems. Or maybe it's just the stuff they sell.

The next day, we all had tickets to watch the New York Yankees. I was like an excited child that morning. We'd all got up bright and early to head out to a local cafe for breakfast. It was an awesome day – the sun was shining and we were going to get to watch one of the most famous sports teams on the planet. You know how kids get all hyperactive on Christmas morning? We were all pretty much like that. Add a couple of cans of Coke to the equation and we were all pretty annoying!

Everyone had finished their breakfasts and there was one slice of toast left on the plate in the middle of the table. I could see Turlough eyeing it up for ages, and it was really bugging me. It was just sat there getting cold and he was hardly being subtle about the way he was looking at it. It must have taken him about 10 minutes to pluck up the

courage to ask if anyone minded if he had the last piece of toast. I was in one of my excitable prankster moods because of the Yankees game and, as far as I was concerned, 10 minutes had been far too long.

Everyone agreed that Turlough could have the toast, and his eyes lit up like he'd found 50p from the tooth fairy under his pillow. Just as he leaned across to grab the object of his desire, I poured my glass of water over the plate, soaking the bread. Everyone's faces flew directly at me. I knew they were torn between laughing and thinking I was a bastard, so I didn't react. I just carried on talking about whatever it was we were talking about. Turl collapsed dejectedly back into his seat.

I don't come across that nice in my stories, do I? I am becoming aware of this fact. It was annoying watching him eye up the toast though. See, I'm weird like that. I get more upset about how someone sips from a bottle than I do about war.

We headed off to the pub for a few and then made our way down to Brooklyn for the game. It was getting hotter and hotter. It was April and I was only in a vest, and even that was too much. I would have gone topless but I'd been called a "Jerk off" by some random American for doing that the day before.

Once in the stadium, we were even more baking. The arena was pretty much an oven. It blocked out any slight breeze so all you were left with was a giant blowtorch of sun straight onto your head.

The game was crap and the Yankees lost 1–0. But it was still an awesome experience because we were sat in the sun with our mates, some ice cold beers and, best of all, we got to watch Taffy's head turn more and more red. Taffy has a bald head and we kept telling him that he should probably cover up. But no, Taffy was a hardened man who was raised on the surface of the Sun. He'd be fine.

After a while we got bored of telling him he'd get sunstroke and instead averted our attention to a very pale, red-haired little girl a few rows in front. She had no sunscreen and nothing covering the back of her neck. That's just bad parenting, we thought, as we watched her singing, "Let's go, Yankees ..."

She was sat with her folks, and the dad was quite a big fellah. We decided it wouldn't be well received if we were to suggest she covered up in this intense sunshine. And that's a liberating feeling. Once you've established there is nothing you can do to prevent a situation, all you can really do is sit back and enjoy watching it unfold. So that's exactly what we did. With the exception of an incredible catch from Derek Jeter, nothing of any excitement was happening on the pitch. So we took our pleasure in a giant baseball serving us Heineken and this young ginger kid getting burned.

"Update lads, she's now started to go pink on the arms. It's spread from the shoulders. Once this hits the neck, we've got some guaranteed sunstroke-induced vomiting."

But still she kept with the "Lets go, Yankees ..." and she'd even thrown in some mini dance-moves with it. She really was enjoying herself. But boy, would she suffer later on.

We liked our sayings in the band back then – like the "You Have" saying I explained before. Well, "Lets go, Yankees" with the little dance became a saying, too. It was a way of stating, "Are you sure? I get the feeling you may regret that in the morning", and it was very fitting for a rock 'n' roll band.

"That slightly plump Goth girl with all the piercings and the fellah with the swastika tattoo said we can sleep at their house tonight if we don't fancy freezing in the bus?"

"Let's go, Yankees!"

After the game, we all headed back to the hostel to get changed and get ready to head into town. Our warnings to Taff had fallen on deaf ears, and now he was struggling. His head looked like a giant strawberry and he was feeling sick. I had sunstroke once in South Africa and it's a pretty grotty feeling. So we put Taffy to bed at the hostel and headed out to grab some beers.

That night, we hammered it completely – it may well have been the biggest drinking session we'd had. If I'm honest, I can't remember very much about it. It's quite hazy but I can remember the odd bullet point. Perhaps if I reel them off, you can put together the night in some way for me? If you could, that would be great because I hate having blank periods of time when I'm pretty certain I was awake.

So, we went out for a few beers. I remember up until about midnight fine. It's just after then that things become a bit blurry.

I recall walking past a massive gang of black street youths and one walking over towards Tim saying something along the lines of, "Yo, white boy. People get killed round here for looking like that." I can't remember what Tim was wearing but I doubt it was anything punishable by death. A T-shirt, jeans and Converse All-Stars was Tim's attire of choice normally. I can't see who would get offended by that particularly.

That's quite a terrifying memory to harbour, actually. I can't remember what our reaction was. I assume we just kept walking and didn't argue back. Well, I'm here, and I'm alive, so I'm certain we just kept walking.

I remember us buying a butt plug from a late-night sex shop. I've never understood the purpose of a butt plug. Is it to keep the arse open, or to keep the arse closed? Is it there to stretch, kind of like wearing in a new pair of shoes, or is it a way to stop any unwanted visitors? I have no idea, but we bought one anyway.

I also have a strange recollection of being in a live-music venue and Barry ejecting someone. He didn't even work there! We were all stood by the main entrance and Barry was chatting up the young lady taking the ticket money. She seemed to be enjoying it, and the rest of us were laughing at some of the lines he was coming out with.

"How long 'til he tells her he's a doorman?" "Ten seconds?" Then she asked him what he did back in England. "I'm a doorman, love." "I made that about three seconds, lads."

All was running smoothly until this big lump of a guy tried to get in. He must have been about 35 years old. He just walked up casually and went to pay the couple of dollars entrance fee.

"Got any ID, mate?" piped up Barry.

What was he doing? He didn't even work there and the guy was clearly much older than 21.

"What? I'm 35, man. Are you kidding?" "Do I look like I'm laughing, mate? No ID – no entry."

The load of us were cracking up and even the woman was laughing. But while the guy rooted around in his wallet for something to prove he was over 21, we all assumed Barry would admit he was joking and let the guy in. But he didn't, he just kept standing there with a stern face. The guy couldn't find anything, so Barry turned him away. And what was funnier was the lady just stood there laughing and let him do it.

Another memory I have is of Turlough in a late-night Subway takeaway. The guy had made up his sub and was asking Turlough what dressings he wanted on it. Turl was in a similar state to the one he was in when he threw coins at the dancer.

"Mayo." "There you go, Sir. Anything else?" "More mayo." "Certainly. There you go." "More mayo." "Umm, okay, Sir." "MORE MAYO."

This must have gone on for ages. All that was left was two soggy bits of bread and a giant pile of mayonnaise, all wrapped up in a Subway bag. When Turl got outside, he opened up the bag and took a bite.

"Too much mayo!" and in the bin it went.

When we stumbled into the hostel, Taffy was still passed out. It doesn't matter how ill you might be, or even if you may have died, you can't pass out around me and Turlough when we're drunk. Out came the pen and out came the camera.

We put the butt plug in Taffy's hand and manoeuvred his arm so he was holding it next to his face. Turlough is a pro when it comes to drawing on passed-out people and has two particular mainstays that get the ball rolling. The first is the nose penis. That's exactly what it says on the tin. The tip of the nose becomes the tip of a penis and the rest is coloured in accordingly. The second regular is the word "C**T!" written across the forehead. After those two are in place, the rest of the masterpiece can be put together around it.

The problem Turlough was having was that because Taffy had a fever, he was sweating out. That meant that the pen wouldn't work properly. Turl was literally carving the word "C**T!" into the forehead of our good friend Taffy.

All the other lads were trying to get Turl to stop. When I say trying, they were lying on their bunks laughing and occasionally going, "Turl ... come on, mate". They were basically doing just as much as we'd done to save the ginger Yankees kid a few hours earlier.

My job was to be the devil on Turlough's shoulder. And the difference between me and the other lads was I took my job seriously. I was holding Taffy still, I was trying to get the pen to work,

I was getting the camera ready – I was being proactive. I think Turl's dark side appreciated that, and we went to town on Taff.

By the time we were done, there wasn't an inch of Taffy's head that didn't either have a penis, a pair of breasts or the word "C**T" on it. We started taking pictures with Taffy's camera. It was one of those disposable ones, which meant he'd have to get the film developed when he got home. We figured the ladies in the photo-developing place deserved a good laugh.

We all eventually passed out, and when we woke up, Taffy was no longer in bed. It turns out that Taff had woken up feeling a lot better and had gone to the shop to get us all some Coke as he always did. Only as he stepped into the courtyard for his morning cigarette, he was greeted with cheers and a flood of laughter from the other residents.

I asked if anyone knew where he was and Tim said he'd heard him scrubbing his face in the bathroom a while earlier. It was mean, but my god was it funny! For us, it got better though.

Barry came in and said that Taffy had gone mad at first but was cool now and had gone round to the shop to get us all some Coke. It was only a prank, so I'm glad Taffy wasn't
too pissed off. After all, it had only been seen by us and a few mates from the hostel. It wasn't like he'd gone to the shop like that. Or, had he?

When Taff returned he looked pretty angry. It turns out that he'd failed to see the big ink penis on the top of his bald patch. So when he was stood in the shop queue, they'd all been in fits of giggles. Poor Taffy had walked all the way to the shop with a giant penis on his head. He was less than amused.

Actually, just talking about it, I remember more about that night than I thought I had! See, this is therapeutic!

When we all got back to England, Taffy had sent the camera to his mum so she could get it developed. We were all pretty skint at that time so any financial help we could get was greatly received. Even if it was just paying the £5 to have some photos developed. Taffy obviously had no idea that we'd loaded up his camera with photos of him. He must have just assumed he'd been a bit trigger-happy and taken more pictures than he'd realised.

When we realised Taffy had sent the camera to his mum, we were mortified. We figured that a woman in her seventies wouldn't take great pleasure in flicking through photos of her son with "C**T" written on his head, a butt plug in his hand and me and Turl posing next to him.

Taffy really milked it and said we'd disappointed his entire family. Weeks later when we saw Leslie and the rest of Taffy's family, they told us how funny it was and how much they'd enjoyed seeing Taffy as a piece of art. That's what I love about the Welsh – they have a sense of humour.

We'd decided that our last full day in New York should be special, so we all headed into Times Square on the subway. Ollie had bought a bunch of red roses and was randomly handing them out to strangers. People get really weird about stuff like that, especially in major cities. Everyone lives this bizarre sheltered life; they can be in a massive crowd of people but acknowledge nobody else's existence. It's quite hard for small-town folks like us to get our heads around. Where we come from, people say "Hello", and welcome interaction. In a place like New York, nobody does anything for anyone else. This is a place where they teach women to scream "FIRE" if they're being attacked because if they scream "RAPE", nobody will help. So, because of that mindset, Ollie handing out roses was met with suspicion. They probably thought they were anthrax-laced or were likely to blow up.

One girl did take a rose, though. A lovely German lady called Anna accepted the gift and said thanks. We were slightly taken aback by her actually talking to us. We invited her out for dinner and she joined us. Anna was studying on Long Island and was just in Manhattan for the day. We got on really well and we've kept in touch and met up in England and Germany since. Anna was the newest member of the group, and so

Turlough, Tim, Ben, Ollie, Taffy, Barry, Passion, Valdis, Anna and I set about getting drunk in Times Square.

Barry was in this amazing mood where the jokes and puns were just falling out of his mouth. Earlier in the day we'd been hassled by some Roman Catholic woman on the train. She took one look at us and clearly thought we needed saving. We were all humouring her and her ramblings for a while but it had started to get annoying. Barry had had enough and just stood up in the middle of the packed carriage and shouted in a Bruce Forsyth voice, "Nice to see you, too see you nice!" and then walked off. The whole carriage just looked at each other, confused. Bruce is a household name in England and that line was one of his old TV show catchphrases, but in the USA he was unheard of. So that line and dramatic voice was lost on the other passengers.

You'd be walking down the street and Barry would just pipe up with "Mind the gap"; so you'd look down for an open manhole or something, only to realise that there was a fat bloke with a GAP jumper coming towards us. That was Barry's humour, and we were all fans.

But that afternoon, Barry taught us the best prank of all. In New York, the streets are about four lanes thick either side. It literally is traffic central. It's also illegal to just skip across whenever you want. I think it's called Jaywalking or something. So you'd have to queue up at a crossing and wait for the "WALK" sign to appear to say it was safe to cross. Now obviously, Manhattan, and Times Square in particular, is crazily busy with tourists and business men and women. So every time you crossed the road, you'd be crossing with about 30-odd other people.

The 10 of us were all stood waiting patiently, and then the "WALK" sign came on and Barry skipped off a few yards ahead. About halfway across the eight lanes, he glanced to his right, shuddered with panic and then legged it over to the other side. Well, in that situation you don't stop to ask questions – your body goes into "fight or flight" mode. Everyone just thought that there must be a car speeding towards us so, without even checking, all nine of us started running as well. Then some bloke flew past me and we realised that every other bugger had started running also. Once we reached the other side, everybody stopped to catch their breath. Strangers were all looking at each other with sheer terror in their eyes, all thanking their lucky stars that the car hadn't hit them. Everyone, that is, apart from Barry, who was just stood chuckling to himself. There had been no car and people were rapidly realising this. I was absolutely shitting myself laughing. That prank got us a treat and it deserved a round of applause. The people in suits, and the Japanese tourists, found it less amusing as they slowly filtered off to go about their day.

We spent the next couple of hours drinking in Irish bars, but between everyone we'd pull the road-crossing prank – each taking it in turns to be the instigator. It worked a treat every time. Pure genius.

The 10 of us went out for a meal that evening and then headed back to Greenwich for a few drinks. Anna was completely a part of our group now and was laughing and joking with all of us. It was strange because we'd only met a few hours before and yet it was like we'd all been friends forever. I guess similar souls gravitate towards each other sometimes. That's a beautiful thing about life and we were very lucky in that respect.

God, I sound like a hippie.

The next day we were flying home, so we figured that a few quiet drinks in a small bar would be a better way to go. There is nothing worse than a long-haul flight with a thumping hangover. We stumbled upon this jazz club in one of the back streets. I can't remember its name but it was everything you'd expect from a jazz club. It was small, smoky and dark.

I can't stand jazz normally, but when you're sat in candlelight, with good company and a few bottles of decent red wine, the music is unimportant. It was chilled-out and that was perfect.

Wine was flowing and flowing, and after a while this quiet night had fallen into the category of "drunken evening". Why did we even bother kidding ourselves? Every night ended up like that so we should have just accepted it. I think that saying: "Let's have a chilled one" was our security blanket for the fact that we were all pretty much alcoholics – some worse than others of course. I'm pretty sure that Turlough and I shared that particular crown.

On the stagger back to the hostel, Ollie spotted this massive canvas on the side of the road. It was a giant painting of something. God knows what it was but it had just been left out on the street. Ollie decided it was probably worth a lot of money and so we should take it back to England and sell it. Drink does bizarre things to people because most of us actually agreed with Ollie and thought that would probably be a good idea.

I'll be honest – it was crap. But then most art these days is crap. Just because it was painted in your own faeces doesn't make it any good. But that's just the way art is now. It's the same with music and films and everything. Fashion over passion. Explosions over a decent plot. So even though this painting was crap, it might be worth something to some rich idiot.

The next morning, we all woke up and Taffy went off and did his usual Coke run. The first thing I spotted was the painting on the floor by the door.

"Hahahahahahahahaha. Ahhhhhahahahahahahaha. It's soooo bad!!!"

It hadn't looked great the night before, but in the cold, sober light of day, it had clearly been done by someone that wasn't the full picnic. Everyone looked at it and had the same reaction. There is no way that that giant piece of crap is coming back on the plane to England!

We all packed up our bags and sat out in the courtyard. We'd have to leave soon and everyone was getting a little bit emotional saying their goodbyes. This trip had been amazing on so many different levels. We'd met some incredible people and, hopefully, they'd enjoyed their New York experience as much as we did. We'd certainly miss them, and these few days in the city that never sleeps would not be forgotten. Well, apart from the bits that I was too drunk to recall earlier.

"So, what do we do with the painting?" "Smash it?"

That's such a boy answer, isn't it? The destructive nature of man. So Tim set up his video camera and Ollie set about smashing the priceless masterpiece over Turlough's head. After two attempts, nothing had happened but a few flakes of paint had come off and Turl had a headache. It really needed a big effort to smash it. It was a massive canvas with a wooden frame. I guess Ollie didn't really want to smash it on his own brother's head.

Barry stepped in. "Give it here."

Turlough backed right off. There was no way he was letting Barry smash it on his head. He kept looking for volunteers but nobody was stepping forward. Then, out of nowhere, a small voice piped up, "Smash it on my head if you want?"

A Welsh lad called Chris had only just arrived at the hostel that morning and was just sat in the corner. We hadn't even been introduced and yet here he was, stepping up to have a painting smashed on his head. So Barry set himself and let rip. BANG!!! The wooden end of the painting smashed straight onto Chris's head. He didn't even flinch. He just shook our hands and went back to sitting on his own in the corner. What the fuck was that about?! What was in it for the lad?!

We grabbed our stuff and left for the airport. That was our New York experience in a nutshell. Smashing a painting on a stranger's head seemed like a fitting way to end it.

You can actually find that video on YouTube if you search: "Priceless Art Smashing, NYC". What's funny is that the video was posted there by Chris himself. What must his friends and family back in Wales have thought of it?

"How you getting on in America, Chris, boyo?"

"Fine, thanks, Dad."

"What you been up to?"

"Just had a gang of big bearded-Englishmen smash a painting on my head."

"What?!"

8: THIS BAND IS THE BOMB

Recording of ' 1981' single, Hoxton Square, London, 2005

Band members:
Gareth Icke - Vocals/Guitar
Tim Pritchard - Guitar
Turlough Ducie - Drums
Ollie Ducie - Bass
Taffy - Roadie/Driver

In July 2005, we had moved on to new management, so our place in Surrey was pulled from underneath us. It was great to be back on the Isle of Wight because we could be around our friends and family; plus, we could all do a bit of cash-in-hand work on the side to help subsidise the band. The only problem was, we were still gigging in London all the time. When you add up the ferry fares, the diesel, the congestion charge and the stupidly expensive parking prices in the city, it was a pretty expensive trip every time.

Our new management wasn't fussed about us bringing in big crowds and playing to hundreds. They simply wanted us put in front of the right people at the right time. And with us, that meant small-but-cool venues, midweek shows and early starts so that the industry people would see us when they came in straight after work. It made sense on that level, I suppose. No top industry people are around at 11 pm on a Saturday night. They have wives and kids and generally live in the suburbs.

Another reason, I think, was to keep us sober. By that time, we had two levels of performance: play sober and play tight and sound great, or get battered and play poorly but put on a hell of a show. I think if we'd managed to find a happy medium, we may have had half a

134

chance. But doing anything by halves simply wasn't in our natures.

We were due to play The Water Rats in Kings Cross on July 6th. I think we were meant to be on stage at about 7.30 pm and play for about 25 minutes – a really shit gig by our standards, but as far as the management was concerned it was time to forget about the masses and get our music into the hands, ears and eyes of the people at the top.

The Water Rats is a small iconic venue in one of the side streets just a hundred yards or so from Kings Cross railway station. It doesn't look much from the outside – just like your average London boozer, sandwiched between two sets of townhouses. When you get inside, it's tiny, dark and covered in torn posters from previous weeks' shows. You

walk through the front door and it's a normal pub, but at the back of the room are two more doors which go through to the actual venue. The band room is no bigger than a Victorian living-room. But it always makes for a great atmosphere.

The way I've described it doesn't really do it justice, but all you need to do is look at what other up-and-coming bands started there and the history speaks for itself. Glasvegas, MGMT, The Rascals – they all started out there.

Another great thing about playing at trendy, historic venues is we never had a problem getting extra people in the van for the journey from the Isle of Wight. We had a nine- seater bus and there were only five of us, so we'd fill the extra seats at £10 each. And then when we got to the venue, we'd let them carry some gear in and tell the promoter they were our roadies. It meant *we* didn't have to carry anything, and *they* got into the gig for free. Everyone's a winner!

On the morning of the 6th, we all met up in the Solent Inn. It was a Wednesday, and we'd all taken a day off from whatever shitty jobs we were doing at the time. There were the five of us in the band, plus our mate, Kev, who helped out with drums, and our other mate, Daz.

Kev had come away with us a bunch of times and I'm pretty sure he gets a few mentions in the other stories. But just in case you don't recall, Kev was about 20 but looked about 12 – a really skinny guy with a shaved head. He wouldn't step outside the door unless he had tracksuit bottoms on and something football-related on his upper half. This guy looked about as much like a musician as Rik Waller looks like a swimwear model; but Christ, could this guy play the drums! Plus, he was actually really good fun to have around. He was basically your very own Fisher Price toy. You just had to press the button and he'd keep you entertained for half an hour.

Daz was a top bloke that I'd known since I was a kid. I think he must have been about 35 back then. He was from York and had that Northern air about him. You know the one. Basically, you think he's going to stab you and then you actually have a conversation and realise that he's your new best friend. Daz was a stupidly intelligent guy that could destroy any university graduate in a test of brain power, but instead chose to be a dad, drink beer and live for football and music. As soon as we said we were playing The Water Rats, he was the first name written on the passenger list.

Bizarrely enough, Daz was also a hairdresser and so would make sure we didn't all look like "footballers" before we went on stage. Our management actually accused me of looking "too much like a footballer". I may have already told you that?

So we're all in the pub having a swift Kronenbourg, when Taffy starts tapping his watch and says in that beautiful broad Welsh accent of his that it's time to go. We spent hours winding up Taffy about how English he sounded and how much he'd lost his Welsh heritage. The truth was, we could probably understand about two in every three words. Enough to grasp a sentence – but only just.

We always had the same routine – get on the boat and get straight to the bar while one of us ran over and commandeered the quiz machine. If anyone managed to get to the quiz machine before us, all hell broke loose. We'd loiter around the machine talking loudly on purpose and saying things like, "Nah, wait about, they'll be done in a minute. They're hardly going to hog the machine for the whole crossing". That would normally be enough to make them play their last 50p and get off.

It sounds like bullying, but so much of what we did in those days was built around routine and superstition. If we couldn't get on that machine, we couldn't have a good show. Everything was out of whack. Weird but true. Musicians are an odd breed, I can promise you.

Taffy would sit drinking his coffee like an adult while the rest of us drank beer and shouted out answers in organised chaos. Normally it ended up with confusion, leading to no answer being pressed and the time meter running out.

GAME OVER.

"Oh, fuck off! I told you it was Turin."

Once we arrived on mainland England, there was always one mission and one mission only.

"Taffy! Find us some booooooze!" We would pull up at the nearest supermarket and stock up on whatever was cheap. Then, off to the motorway we'd go.

We were pretty easily pleased, to be honest. As long as we had a beer in our hand and some decent tunes on the stereo, we would happily sit in traffic for hours. Taffy, on the other hand, was the one doing all the work. He hated London with a passion and was often one step away from a giant heart-attack every time he drove there.

This trip was different though, to be fair, and it was all plain sailing. We were heading into London during rush hour – the very time when every other person is heading out of London.

We arrived at the venue, pulled the old "These two are our roadies" trick, and we were all set.

I reckon we must have played to about 20 people that night, which seems pointless, but, like I said, the management would rather have had 20 industry people than 200 drunken partygoers. Personally, I would have much preferred the latter. I never got into this to try to impress Mr Big Cheese. None of us did – we just wanted to bang out some tunes and have a laugh.

I can't really tell you much about the show. It was all pretty boring: get up, play five songs to hardly anyone, then walk off stage, shake a few hands, swap a few business cards and get back onto the bus. It's wasn't exactly the gig of the century, but we had travelled all that way and we had spent all that money, so sod it. We were getting plastered. We loaded up the bus with our gear, said our goodbyes and headed off back home to our Island. It must have only been about 9 pm, but that meant we would be catching the 1 am boat and we wouldn't get to bed until 2.30 am. We were going to feel like shit in the morning either way, so we may as well enjoy it.

"Taffy! Find us some booooooze!!!"

In and around Kings Cross there are tonnes of corner shops and Eastern European off-licences. I really don't get the Polish food. Most of it looks like it once belonged to part of a human. But when it comes to beer, the Poles and the Czechs know what they're doing. We filled the van full of foreign beer and hit the road.

When you're heading out of London, there *is* no quiet time on the roads. All you're certain of is that a black car with blacked-out windows will at some point cut you up, and that you'll probably have to pull over at least three or four times to allow a speeding police car to fly past you. It's the beauty of city life – a beauty that makes me content to live on my Island.

Taffy was getting more and more annoyed with the length of time it was taking us to get out of London, and, I'm sure, getting more and more annoyed with how drunk and loud we were all getting in the back. One thing that drunkenness on high-percentage lager does to men is make them think that nudity is a good idea. So, first the shirts are coming off and being swung above our heads; then windows are being opened and things are being shouted at passers-by; then the music is turned up and everyone is up dancing. We're still in a busy built-up area, remember!

The bus pulled up at a red light somewhere in South East London. There was a Sainsbury's local with a large group of girls stood outside. They obviously can't miss us. We're a bloody big white bus with "www.kody.co.uk" emblazoned on the side; *there's Reach Out I'll Be There by The Four Tops* blaring out; and there are six half-naked men dancing at them. I dread to think who they thought we were. Certainly not a band, I'm sure. More like a Wednesday night gay-parade through the streets of London. They were probably expecting us to start handing out condoms and leaflets about sexual health.

The girls started wolf-whistling at us. Well, that's like a red rag to a drunken bull. All of us, in unison, whipped off our trousers and pants. Now we're six blokes, totally naked, dancing to the Four Tops in front of a large group of now-terrified women. I'm pretty sure there are plenty of laws against that kind of behaviour.

The lights changed to green, and Taffy stepped on it.

We were all still stood up, so as soon as the bus pulls away, the load of us are sent tumbling into one giant naked heap on the bus floor. It's not something I've repeated since, I must add.

So, we get back to the Isle of Wight. Usual drill on the boat, only this time nobody's shouting anything at the quiz machine because everybody is too totally battered to speak properly. Occasionally, someone will muster the energy to hit a button and hope it's the right one. It rarely was, and so pound after pound went into that quiz machine slot, never to be seen again – at least not by us anyway.

The following morning I'm lying in what can only be described as my "pit", still fully clothed and covered in water. I always take a pint of water to bed to try to avoid a hangover. I guess that night I must have missed my mouth. It wasn't the first time that had happened. Or the last.

I was woken up by Turlough phoning me.

"Hello?!"

"Have you seen the news, man?!"

"No, I'm asleep. Well, not asleep. I was asleep."

"London's been bombed."

When he said that, all I could think of was the Blitz. I wasn't thinking bombs on tube trains or buses – I was thinking the Luftwaffe. Which is odd, I know. But I was hungover. The mind needs time to adapt to consciousness.

I flicked on the news and there it was – the London bombings of 7th July, 2005. Fifty-six people killed in separate bomb attacks across the city. It's one of those things that define a generation. See, I remember my mum saying that about the JFK assassination of 1963. She can remember exactly where she was when that happened. But we'd already had ours on 11th September four years earlier. I wasn't expecting another one of those moments. But here it was.

On the screen came footage of Kings Cross tube station. I was thinking, "Shit, we were just parked there!"

I got up, showered, and headed straight down to The Solent. It's the place you go when things happen. If anyone famous that we actually respected died, we went and had a beer for them in The Solent. It was basically a ritual that made us feel better about drinking heavily on a weekday. Once, a whale died and washed up on our local beach. We went and raised a glass to the animal's spirit. It didn't take much of an excuse.

The band and a handful of the locals were all sat about having a few beers and talking about what had happened. You'd get the odd uneducated, "Those bloody Muslims" comment from one of the older gentlemen. We kept our mouths shut. They were from the older generation, and there was no point wasting your breath trying to convert them to accept that perhaps they shouldn't just swallow the version of events fed to them on "The News". Our generation is much more open to asking questions. Older folks tend to get high-and-mighty, "Queen and country", and get defensive when confronted with anything they perceive to be anti-English.

But this was a monumental moment in recent history, and, whatever your stance was on the matter, fifty-six innocent people had lost their lives. It was a huge tragedy and one that we sort of felt involved with in a strange way. We'd been right there just a few hours earlier. We'd bought beers from a shop just outside that station. What if that guy who sold us beer and put up with our drunken jokes was one of the fifty-six? All those thoughts go through your head and it becomes more personal to you. Little did we know that two weeks later it would become very personal to us.

Okay, where was I? In the Solent Inn, chatting with mild-mannered racists.

Cracking on ... About a week later, we were due to start recording our two-track single at Miloco Studios in Hoxton Square, London. We'd somehow managed to secure the producing skills of a guy called Simon Hanhart. This guy was top of his game and it was a real coup for us to work with him. We'd had a few meetings and we knew that we were going to be worked insanely hard, but the results would be incredible. None of us was scared of hard work so we'd really prepared the songs and paid attention to every little detail. Obviously you pay by the hour in a recording studio so everything we could iron out before we went "on the clock" would be a real bonus.

The night before we were due to start recording, we got on the boat, played the quiz machine and drove up to Mitcham in Surrey. Staying in London was a no-go because of the cost; and sleeping in the bus in London was also out of the question. To be honest, it probably would have been cheaper to have paid for a hotel than it would to have fed the parking meter for four days.

Turlough and Ollie's auntie and uncle lived in Mitcham and they'd offered to put us up. It meant we'd just need to make the drive to Shoreditch and back each day. It's a pretty straightforward route through Streatham, Stockwell, Elephant & Castle, and across the river.

We'd arrived in Mitcham sober. No beer had flowed on the journey at all – which wasn't like us but we were taking this seriously; we had a big day tomorrow and we didn't want to arrive at the studio with hangovers and looking rough.

We pulled into a housing estate, not unlike the one featured in _Only Fools and Horses_, only slightly more upmarket. We were greeted by an argument between two men. One was about five-foot-six with a beer belly, and wearing a vest; and the other guy was a black fellah about six-foot-three and of pretty large build. All we heard was the shorter guy say, "I've never seen a black man with a black eye but I fucking will if I don't get my money!"

It's up there with: "So, the guy's wife came flying out of the tent, chucked a can of beans at me and then started eating a unicycle" on the list of sentences you never expect to hear.

We all looked at each other – Turlough and Ollie both laughing hysterically.

The black man turned and walked away, and the shorter guy welcomed us in. He was Turlough and Ollie's uncle. "Welcome in, lads. Let's get you a cider!"

Well it's rude to turn down hospitality, isn't it? A couple of hours later we were all smashed on scrumpy and ready to hit the hay. Turlough and I always shared a bed. Wherever we stayed we always ended up bunking up together. I think it's because we were both in long-term relationships and actually liked having someone else in the bed. We'd often wake up in each others arms. But that's normal for two six-foot-tall bearded men in their early twenties, isn't it?

Anyway, we took the bedroom on the top floor, Tim and Ollie took the living room on the middle floor and Taffy slept in a spare room on the ground floor. Everyone was starting to fall asleep apart from me and Turlough. We had got to that level of drunkenness where we became about nine years old. I kept recording videos of me and Turlough speaking in a fake Welsh accent saying things like, "Awwww Cwmbran" and, "Ahhhh, there's Abergavenny", and then we sent them to Taffy. We could hear his phone ringing over and over. We knew Taffy would snap eventually so we locked the door.

Just a few videos later we could hear him bounding up the stairs, and he tried to break in. "Will you just fuck off sending videos!"

"Sorry, Taffy."

We weren't sorry. We'd just seen him furious and thought it best to apologise.

Turl and I were still up for pranks but realised we'd probably pushed Taffy as far as we could push him. We had taken a pint of water to bed each, and, though we knew we'd probably feel hungover if we didn't drink them, we'd sacrifice them in the name of comedy. We opened the door and sneaked down to the middle floor. Ollie and Tim were snoring away with their mouths wide open. I'd got the giggles which is the worst thing because the more you try to be quiet, the louder you become.

We were just hatching the plan as Ollie and Tim both opened their eyes at the same time. Turl and I panicked, tossed the water clean in their faces and bolted up the stairs.

Tim and Ollie were up and at us pretty quickly. I flew through the bedroom door and onto the bed. Turlough was in soon after me and slammed the door shut just as Ollie piled into it. There was a massive bang. Pure chaos ensued.

The next morning, we were all up bright and early – which was surprising given the amount of cider we'd drank, and the pranks of the night before. I think it was all the excitement of actually recording in a top London studio with a top producer. Plus, it was a blistering hot summer's day. It's always easier to motivate yourself when the sun is shining.

We all bundled into the bus and made the drive up into London. We'd piled through Streatham, past Stockwell, past Oval and up into the Hackney Road area and to Hoxton Square. You're probably wondering why I'm telling you this again, but it is important that you store this information. Its importance becomes apparent later on.

We arrived at Hoxton Square. If you haven't been there, it's basically the cool and "happening" part of London. There is a small park surrounded by bars and restaurants and music venues, and, obviously, the recording studio.

Every city has one of these areas. It used to be poor and rundown, so musicians, poets, artists and film writers would all flock there to live because it was cheap. Now while the creative people are poor and don't make much money from their art, they are cool. So then all the rich, boring banker-types with no personalities start to flock to the area to become cool by association. Now once the people with money come in, so do the swanky wine bars and the redevelopment. The house prices go up, the artists can't afford to live there anymore and so move on to the next cheap area. All you're left with is posh wine bars, accountants in suits drinking champagne and, perhaps if you're lucky, a plaque somewhere that bears the name of a recently deceased rock star. Hoxton Square was on the turn at this point. It was starting to become "trendy", but, at that time anyway, still held some of its authenticity.

All we had was a postcode. We had no building number for the studio at all. We drove around Hoxton for a few minutes before Taffy pipes up with, "Ahh, Miso! There it is!"

"Taffy, mate, that's a noodle bar."

"Oh."

Eventually, we called the studio and an engineer came out to meet us. The studio was called "Miloco" and it had a small entrance-door next to the noodle bar. Taffy had been close, but the tonne of Chinese people eating with chopsticks was probably a clue that it wasn't a recording studio.

We loaded all of our gear into the studio and parked up the bus in the Square. We would record from 10 am until 6 pm for four days. Hoxton Square charges £4 per hour to park there. So, doing the maths quickly, that's £128 in parking charges. Sod that! Taffy got back in the bus and drove off to find us somewhere free to park.

The studio was amazing! You walked through one door into a massive courtyard. It had tables and chairs laid out in the sunshine. Then you went through another door into the studio itself. It was real state-of-the-art. We were all looking at each other like we'd finally made it.

I spent the day getting the tempos and laying down the guide tracks for the three songs. If you don't know what that is, basically you'll get the speed that the song should be and then you get beeps in your headphones at that tempo. You play and sing the song keeping to that tempo, and then everyone else puts their parts on top of the guide track. At the end, you take out the guide track, record better vocals and it's job done. It's probably more complex than that but you get the picture.

I'd laid down my parts and now Turlough was in there starting to lay down the drum tracks. Yet Taffy had only just got back from parking the bus.

"Where did you park, Taff? Birmingham?"

Turns out Taff had driven for miles and managed to find a place to park way up in North London. He then had to get a bus all the way back to us in Hoxton Square. That's serious dedication to not having to pay parking fees!

This was the summer when England finally beat Australia in the Ashes. I don't think we'd beaten them since 1981 or something stupid like that. Apart from Ollie, none of us was really into cricket – but we were into England. I remember an old Ricky Gervais show on XFM. I think we'd just won the Rugby World Cup and he said that he hated rugby, but that he'd watch England win anything. We were pretty much the same. Then I think Gervais went on to say that he never used to like war until he realised we were so bloody good at it. That's one thing we have in common – we all love Gervais.

We all wanted to watch the cricket, so we dragged the TV out of the studio and into the courtyard. While Turlough was laying down his drum tracks, the rest of us sat in the sunshine drinking ice-cold Coke and watching England demolish the Aussies. See, most of our friends were at work and here we were chilling in the sunshine. The amount of times we'd get older lads back home saying stuff like, "When are you going to get a real job?" In answer to that, I'll get a real job when I get bored of this lifestyle. And I can't see that happening anytime soon!

So, this was our life. I'd be needed occasionally for my opinion on a certain drum roll or a certain bass part but, all in all, Turlough, Ollie and Tim were on the ball and just got on with laying down their parts. Apart from a couple of hours of laying down rhythm guitar, I wasn't really needed until the last day when I'd lay down my vocals.

What a life! We'd get up in the morning, drive to London, Taff would go to park the van while the lads recorded their parts, and I sat, Coke in hand, watching cricket in the sunshine. You can't buy a lifestyle like that. Well, actually, maybe you can, but never mind. I'd literally only rise from my seat if England took a wicket. I'd run into the studio and punch the air, so that whoever was supposed to be concentrating on recording would know we'd taken another wicket. It was probably extremely off-putting but I never really thought about that at the time.

I was just sitting in the sunshine, when all of a sudden a police helicopter appeared at what felt like just a few metres above my head. Stuff was blowing all over the courtyard. Paper, empty Coke cans, whatever was lying around. I was wondering what the hell was going on when Tim came flying out of the studio on his phone. "There's been another bomb attack!"

We all ran outside the studio and into Hoxton Square. It was pretty obvious from the position of the helicopter that something was kicking off near to where we were. As soon as we got out onto the street there was chaos. People were all running under the railway bridge and towards the Hackney Road. I don't know why, but we all ended up running after them as well. As we passed under the bridge and around the corner, there were police everywhere. The whole of the Hackney Road was cordoned off and in the middle was an abandoned bus. It was one of the old red ones that they love to sell replicas of to tourists. The only difference between this one and the poor imitations was that this one no longer had windows.

The whole scene was far too much for some people, and many were crying and hugging each other. We lads didn't really feel any emotion. Not fear or panic or anything. I think that coming from a small island shelters you from stuff like that. We were probably in such a state of shock that we were rendered numb. We asked one of the police officers if anyone was hurt, and he said No. Apparently, only the detonator had gone off and not the actual bomb. As soon as this information started circulating through the crowd, the tears turned into cheers.

A few local lads had gone home and got a stereo system, and the off-licence was packed. People were celebrating. "We are London and we ain't scared of nobody!" was being shouted randomly among the masses. We knew we weren't getting any more recording done today. Not with all the helicopters and noise going off around the studio. So we thought: If you can't beat them – join them. We piled into the shop and stocked up on beer. The music we were dancing to was bloody dreadful, but we didn't care. It was all about being here and making a stand. I don't know who was responsible for those bombs or if it was just a fear-mongering tactic to bring about more terror laws. But what I do know is that it made a city once divided, in to a city as one. If only for that day, it didn't matter what your background was, where you were raised, the colour of your skin or your tax bracket – you were London. We were London.

After a while, we headed up to pick up the bus. There was no way that we were going to be able to get the bus into Hoxton Square, so we stocked up on beer and headed out. It took forever to get down to Mitcham as so many roads were closed and blocked off. It probably would have been easier to have driven all the way out of London and got onto the M25 and circled the entire city. But instead we sat for hours in traffic, drinking beer and listening to very loud, very good, music.

We finally got back to Surrey and the day's events took their toll. All five of us were passed out in bed in no time. I almost felt privileged to have been part of those events. I know that seems like a weird thing to say, and had anyone been killed or badly hurt I certainly wouldn't be feeling like that. But like I said earlier about the moments that define generations, it felt like we'd been part of one of those moments on the streets of Shoreditch.

The next morning we made the journey into London as normal. Only this time, as we passed by Stockwell Station it was teeming with police.

"What the fuck is going on now?!"

We were redirected away from the area and so once again found ourselves lost in the maze that is London. Even satellite navigation hasn't got a clue in London. In fact, it wouldn't surprise me if the lady that does the sat-nav voice-over started asking pedestrians for directions. "Pull over and ask this gentleman for directions."

When we finally got to the studio we were greeted by the producer, Simon. "Have you heard about that lad at Stockwell?"

We hadn't heard anything. The police had just directed us away but not explained why.

"Nope."

"Apparently, he ran away from some coppers so they shot him."

Do we live in the Middle East now or something? He ran off, so they _shot_ him? Next they'll be stoning women to death for burning their husbands' egg and chips. All I could think of was the amount of times as a kid that I ran away from the police. In fact, if we were bored we'd often see a pair of coppers, shout "Shit! Quick!" and then run off just to get them to chase us. We'd never done anything wrong, and if they caught us we'd just say that we realised we were late home for tea. I wouldn't have wound up the police if I'd thought I'd get a bullet in the head.

It turns out the poor fellow was a young Brazilian by the name of Jean Charles de Menezes, who was guilty of absolutely nothing and had about as much to do with the July 7 attacks as Princess Diana did.

We all got on with recording again and tried to block the previous day's events – and indeed that morning's events – out of our minds. We were recording two tracks that would hopefully take us to the next level. There had been some industry interest from our live shows so now we had to back it up with a recording of quality. The main single was a song called _1981_, and the B-side was a track called _After Today_. They were equally strong, and it was a bit of a flip-the-coin job to decide which one would be the main single and which one would be the B-side.

That day's recording session had gone really well and now I was locked away in the vocal booth laying down the vocals. All the guys were out in the courtyard chilling out with a few beers. They'd done their parts so they deserved to relax. After a while, I stepped out for a break. Everyone was standing in silence.

"What's going on?" I asked. It literally was like a bunch of lads stood around their best mate's grave.

"Taffy's mum's house has been raided by the police," said Tim. Taffy looked close to tears and I really couldn't understand what the hell was going on.

Taffy's mum was in her seventies. Why on earth would they be raiding *her* house?

Taffy explained that the bus was registered at her address in Wales as he didn't have a permanent address on the Isle of Wight.

I still wasn't grasping it. What would the police want with Taffy's mum, and what did our bus being registered there have to do with the police at all?

Then all was explained.

In times of war, or, in this case, "terror", people are urged to keep their eyes open and ears to the ground and to report any unusual activity. The problem with that is that very often common sense is overlooked. One such person in North London had looked so far beyond common sense, they couldn't see woods or trees or anything even resembling timber.

Taffy had been driving off up to a residential area where he could park up the bus for free. One nosey neighbour in that area had got wind of this and called the police. Now, bearing in mind our bus was a giant white thing with our website in *massive* letters painted on the sides, the neighbour could have quite easily typed in the website, seen we were a band and seen that our headline's page stated that we were recording our single in London that day. Problem solved. But that would have been too easy.

Instead, they phoned the police and reported that this bus had only arrived the day before the bomb attack and would come and go at the same time everyday for three days. They also stated that the driver was a stocky, dark-skinned fellow who wore army-style clothing. Basically, a five-foot Welshman who had caught the sun over the summer and wore combat trousers was now made to sound like Osama bin Laden's right-hand man.

The police then went through security-camera and CCTV footage of the van's daily journey. And lo and behold, it took in Oval, Stockwell and that entire route up into the centre of town before veering off onto the Hackney Road and heading up to this residential area.

That was enough in the Metropolitan Police's minds to dispatch the

Welsh police to storm an elderly woman's house and kick down her front door.

According to Taffy's mum, they kept shouting, "Where is he? Where is he?"

Well, that just shows the level of intelligence we are dealing with. The police are there because he's in London, and yet they're asking where he *is?* What's terrifying is that – stupid or not – the police have guns, and as that morning's situation with Jean Charles de Menezes had proved, they weren't scared to use them.

So here we all were, stood in the courtyard of a top London studio where we were meant to be making what was supposed to be our "big break single", and instead we're all stood in a huddle, shitting ourselves.

Taffy had collected the bus and it was now parked outside the studio on Hoxton Square. It was only a matter of time before a PC spotted it and reported it. Tim and I were urging Taffy to phone the police.

"Just call them up, explain the situation and it will be fine."

We assumed that a couple of coppers would turn up, take a look at the van, come in and have a chat with us in the studio, maybe even have a cup of tea, and then be on their way. But in this new world of terror and fear-mongering, all sense of rationality went out of the window.

Taffy called the police and agreed to be sat in the van when they arrived. He went out and sat in the van while we all stood outside in the doorway.

Within seconds the place was teeming with police. "Put your hands on the steering wheel!" yelled one gun-wielding officer. "Keep your hands where we can see them!" shouted another. Taffy was told to slowly climb out of the bus with his hands on his head.

"They're gonna fucking kill him," I said. I honestly thought they were going to. They were waving guns around with the kind of animation you'd find in a primary-school game of Cowboys and Indians. Every now and then a gun would swing around and point in our direction. In complete Britney Spears dance-routine choreography, all our hands would go up in the air in unison. It must have looked hilarious to an outsider, and I can almost raise a smile about it now. But at the time all we could think about were the seven bullets that had just been fired into an innocent Brazilian man's head.

Just when it seemed like the chaos was going to spill over, and the disorganised yells of several undertrained coppers would lead to one shaky trigger-finger shaking a little too much, it all calmed down. Literally like some hypnotist had clicked his fingers, and bang ... all went quiet.

One of the senior officers spoke to Taffy and all was resolved within minutes. What on earth was the point of all that?! Why not just have an adult conversation and leave John Wayne and his mates in the police van?

I've found several times in my life that there is nothing more desperate than an embarrassed policeman. They will search for anything to end the whole debacle with them on top. Basically, they've fucked up. We're a rock band from the Isle of Wight – about as far away from extremist terrorists as you can get. Yet, instead of apologising for the misunderstanding and saying, "Yeah, lads, sorry about the whole gun-pointing thing" and then offering to buy us all new underwear, they tried to find problems with the bus. They checked every single detail of Taffy's licence, of the MOT certificate, of the insurance details, even down to the deepness of the tread on the tyres – all of which were completely in order, of course. Taffy kept a tight ship. There was no way that PC Plod was getting us on that.

They all piled back into their cars and vans and cleared off. And that was that. But not once did Taffy's mum receive an apology or any money to pay for a new door or anything. Not even some flowers as a token "sorry for stormtrooping your lovely home". Nothing.

We managed, despite all the craziness and complications, to finish the recording. It came out great, and we were all totally over the moon with it. That night after I'd finished the vocals, I'd ran out to the bus to grab a stash of beers we kept in the back. You can't finish a record and not have a few celebratory beers. Plus, Simon, the producer, had been locked away in the studio this whole time. At least we'd got to have a break so we could dance near blown-up buses and have guns pointed at us. Simon hadn't had any of these relaxing experiences. He deserved a beer.

As I stepped outside, there was a large gang of black fellahs surrounding a Mercedes with blacked-out windows. I wouldn't normally notice the colour of anyone's skin as it really isn't important. Only on this occasion I turned to glance at where this god-awful music was blaring from, to be greeting with:

"What da fuck you lookin' at, white boy?" Brilliant.

Like we haven't had enough drama for a lifetime in the last couple of days? I just ignored him and walked over to the bus. I grabbed the beers and stomped back to the studio door. Unfortunately, this meant I had to walk past the front of their car again.

"I said what you lookin' at, white boy?" I wasn't even looking that time! I'd learned from my previous mistake. I'm a quick learner. But as much as I'm a quick learner, I'm not great at ignoring people when they're attempting to start some kind of argument, and I'm not a huge fan of racism no matter who it is. So I turned to the car, put my free hand across my mouth and let out a giant yawn. The guy's eyes opened wide in disbelief. "Boring mate, boring," I said as I reached for the door handle, praying that it was unlocked. If it hadn't been, I'd have been up shit creek. But thankfully it was open, and I skipped inside and locked it firmly behind me.

I walked back into the courtyard where the guys were all standing. "Might wanna hold off going outside for a bit."

So we all sat in the courtyard drinking lukewarm Heineken and listening to the tracks we'd recorded. They weren't mixed properly and they hadn't been mastered or any of that fancy bollocks but we all knew we were onto something special. The songs just sounded a million times better than anything we'd done before. Normally I'd need one hundred per cent concentration in a recording studio. I'd need to focus on what I was doing and try to get the best out of myself. But with this recording, I don't think I'd thought about it once. I'm pretty sure the guys were the same. We'd almost let our subconscious do the recording while our conscious minds were distracted with thoughts of bombs and guns and helicopters. It's not a recording technique I'd like to repeat, but it certainly worked for us in this scenario.

An hour or so later, I took a peek out of the front door. The lads in the noisy car had cleared off so we were safe to pack up the bus and head back to the Isle of Wight. The car could have been waiting around the corner and could perform a drive-by at any moment. I'd had a few Heinekens by then so I wasn't overly bothered. Heineken makes you think that you're Neo from *The Matrix* and that you can dodge bullets. Or maybe that's just me.

Taffy was the king of loading the bus. He had his technique and nobody would dare get in the way of it. It was ingenious though. I reckon he could load the entire contents of a five-bedroom house into a Ford Cortina if you gave him enough time. So we would lug the gear outside and drop it next to the bus. He'd then load it in his magical way and we'd be all set. Only this time, Taffy didn't need to unlock the door as it was already swinging open.

"FOR FUCK'S SAKE!!" shouted Taffy. "I DON'T NEED THIS SHIT!!"

The inside of the bus was completely trashed. Someone had broken in and had taken anything they could find. Luckily for us, all our musical equipment had been in the studio so that was fine. But they'd taken the sat nav and the stereo; but not the whole stereo, no – that would have been smart. Instead, they'd just taken the front. That rendered it useless to them and useless to us. We were completely insured so we only really had to worry about getting out of London without the sat nav and having to travel home without any music. Then, once home, we'd claim and get our stuff replaced. Then Taffy realised they'd stolen his toolkit. This was Taffy's pride and joy and was left to him when his father passed away. The insurance would replace the tools but not the actual tools his father used. They were priceless, and Taffy was distraught.

It was pretty obvious who it was that had done it and Ollie and I were in no mood to beat around the bush. Taffy phoned the police and I told him to describe the car and the gang of lads; they'd definitely done it. Tim and Turlough weren't so convinced and even hinted that it might be racist to assume that the lads around that car were guilty.

"It's nothing to do with fucking race. It's to do with who robbed our fucking bus!" Ollie and I were not best impressed and the idea of a vigilante mission was becoming more and more appealing.

The police said they'd call us back. We had a ferry to catch, so we drove back through the maze that is London and tried to find our way home. We sat in silence, and Taffy was visibly fuming.

After a couple of hours, still nothing from the police. If you phone up and accuse a rock band of being Al-Qaeda, however, the police are there in a second trying to shoot up the place.

Eventually, they called back. The robbery had already been reported by a couple of Eastern European lads. They'd seen a load of lads with a black Mercedes break into our bus and start helping themselves. With no thought for their own safety, the two lads had chased them off. I guess that's why they only had time to get half of the stereo. So we were right about who had done it. But instead of saying "I told you so" or gloating, I just took pleasure in the fact that there are still people out there who are willing to help others.

Those two blokes couldn't get Taffy's toolkit back or replace our sat nav, but the fact that they were outnumbered and still put themselves on the line to help their fellow man was something to take comfort from.

I think that's what we all gained from that bizarre few days. We got a great recording out of it but, more than that, we got to be part of something bigger than ourselves – a distinct part of London history.

9: WANKEST BIRTHDAY EVER

East Molesey, Surrey 2005

Band members:
Gareth Icke - Vocals/Guitar
Tim Pritchard - Guitar
Turlough Ducie - Drums
Ollie Ducie - Bass
Taffy - Roadie/Driver

You okay, mate? I haven't totally weirded you out yet? I hope not. I'm quite enjoying rambling all of this to you. If I had a shrink, they'd probably think it was therapeutic for me to share. Mind you, you could well need their card when I'm done with you.

Okay.

It must have been November, 2005. I would have been about 23 or so. We were all living in one room at our mate Lance's flat in East Molesey. It's right next to Hampton Court in the posh outskirts of London. It was pretty cramped, but it was awesome. Living there was definitely the best time we had in the band. Everything was positive and everyone was feeling great about where this band would eventually take us. Some of the gigs weren't even that great; but they didn't need to be. *We* believed, and so did everyone around us.

Just a few weeks before, we were all living in our separate places on the Isle of Wight doing shitty jobs to pay the rent and then occasionally playing a show here and there. But now we were based just outside London where we were starting to get a following. The best part of it all was that we were all together. We hadn't let the pressure of achieving success get to us yet. We were just five mates hanging out, drinking beer and playing songs. What more could you want? I think the saying is: "Find a job you love and you'll never have to work a day in your life". That summed it all up for us back then.

Lance's flat was on the main road above a motorbike shop. You went upstairs and there was a kitchen, a bathroom and a bedroom. Then there were some more stairs that led to the living room. That was our new home. It wasn't massive, but you pay for location in that area. For the amount that flat probably cost, you'd get a four-bedroom detached house with a garden and a garage back on our little island.

Let me try to describe what our front room looked like. Umm, you know if you watch the news when there has been a mass genocide somewhere, they'll show all the body-bags lying in a row? Well, picture that horror scene and you've basically got what anyone would witness if they walked into that front room before about 10 am. Only we affectionately named our body bags "sleeping bags".

There was one small sofa, but Tim took that. So Turlough, Ollie, Taffy and I all lined up on the floor in our body bags. I didn't mind, as my spine is in a similar condition to the spine of a 95-year-old traffic-accident victim. I need hard floors. Confession: I'm 29 and I still sleep on a futon. If I sleep on a normal bed for longer than a couple of nights, I struggle to walk. I'm a cripple, but my liver still functions – which is surprising. I probably shouldn't tempt fate when it comes to my liver.

So, let me describe the room because it's important you imagine the scene. You walk up the stairs, minding your head on the low ceiling. If you look up, you'll see a dent about the same shape and size as my head. I learned to mind my head the hard way. I learn most things the hard way. I learned not to call a doorman a "dickhead" in a similar, head-injury-based way.

You walk into the room. It's in the roof so the ceiling is slanted and has those fancy skylight things. On the left side is a sofa, and in the far right corner is a TV. Look to the floor and all you can see are sleeping bags and pillows. It looks like a homeless shelter after a natural disaster. You know when the local school opens up it s gymnasium to hundreds of people whose homes have floated away? There is a mass of duvets and blankets? Yeah – like that. Then pan round to the right and there is another TV with a PlayStation set up. The walls are covered in posters of The Who – thanks to Lance's obsession with the band. Then, if you turn again so you're looking back towards the stairs, you'll see a pile of Coke cans that is about eight deep, eight along and about twelve cans high. That's the room.

So you have a mental image, right?

Well, basically, every day was the same. Taffy would get up stupidly early because he was still on an army body-clock; he'd run into town and get breakfast ingredients and a 12-pack of Coke. He'd come back and serve us all breakfast as we slowly woke from our booze-induced slumber. For some reason, Taff had an obsession with putting five-spice powder and garlic cloves in the baked beans. I never fully understood what that was all about, but we scoffed it down just the same. When somebody has cooked you a fry-up, you don't question it. Well, maybe you do but you wait about six years. I'll question it now. Who puts bloody garlic cloves in baked beans?!

Then, Taff and Tim would sip tea like two civilised old folks while Turlough, Ollie and I polished off the 12-pack of Coke. Tim can't drink Coke as it gives him what we affectionately called "windy pops" – the shits.

I hadn't realised why my dentistry bills were so high until I told you that; it explains an awful lot. And I dread to think what my stomach lining is like – I doubt I have any left.

Like I said, every day was generally the same – except this morning was different. It was Ollie's birthday and we'd planned to have a night out in Kingston upon Thames. Kingston is a vibrant town just a 10-minute cab ride from where we were staying. It's basically as cool and as busy as London, but because it's based around university students, the drinks are about half the price. The thing you learn about England is that if a place has "upon Thames" after it, it normally means you'll need to remortgage your wife and kids to pay for a hot chocolate. Luckily, because of the students, Kingston was cheaper.

Our mate, Kev, had piled up the night before so the six of us were planning a lazy day of booze and PlayStation, followed by a heavy night out in Kingston; your industry- standard birthday, really. I've mentioned Kev before, haven't I? Young skinny guy; awesome drummer.

So, after Taffy's alarm clock rang, Turlough, Ollie and I – grudgingly sharing a Coke or two with Kev – all got showered and dressed and piled into town. We were heading to get all the beers stocked up and ready for the day. For some reason, at the time we had an obsession with Snakebite & Black. If you don't already know, Snakebite & Black is a shandy made with equal parts of lager and cider and a splash of blackcurrant cordial. It gets you absolutely battered. But aside from that, it was made illegal back on the Isle of Wight and so pubs had to stop serving it. If I'm honest, that was probably the only reason we drank so much of it. Rebelling against the tiniest of things made us feel big back then. I think we thought we were James Dean or something. "What you rebelling against?"

"What you got?"

Recently, Tim found a load of old Kody stuff in a box in his garage. Inside the box was a tonne of old junk, set-lists and gig posters. But for some reason he'd kept the receipt from one of our past visits to Tesco in East Molesey. It read: 4 x 3 litre bottles of Frosty Jack's white cider; 18 cans of Carlsberg lager; 2 x 1 litre bottles of Robinsons blackcurrant squash; 1 x loaf of white bread; cheese.

Jesus, we were healthy back then. The receipt just says: "Our plan is to get really drunk, and eat something which, even in our drunken state, we couldn't fuck up."

We got back home and Tim got on barman duties, dishing out Snakebites all round.

We'd set up Tim's TV and PlayStation console and started a round-robin tournament on Pro Evolution Soccer. In those days there were two big football computer games – "Pro Evo" or "FIFA". No one ever played both – you had to choose. It was like Blur or Oasis, Coke or Pepsi. Pick one and stick with it. Well, Turlough and I were firmly in the FIFA camp but the others were nailed to the Pro Evo side. What that meant was that after two or three games, Turlough and I were pretty much out of the competition for honours and were, therefore, bored. If we'd taken FIFA along, they'd have only got funny and

refused to play it. Though, I must say, Tim is now a FIFA believer. They all come to the dark side eventually. That's not really important.

The other lads were all playing their competitive games while Turlough and I just sat on the sofa and got down to drinking. After a while, we went rooting around Lance's DVD collection to try to find something to put on the other TV. At least then we could watch a film or something while the others were playing on the computer.

All we could find was old videos and DVDs of The Who. Literally every gig, live-TV performance and interview that the band EVER did was piled up in Lance's living room. I'm sure there was probably even secret camera-footage of one of them walking their dog. But no movies ... except for one.

I can't remember the name, but it was something German and it had naked women on the cover. I'm no rocket scientist, but my money was on it being porn.

Turl and I thought it would be funny to whack it on the other TV with the sound off, to see how long it took the others to notice that someone was getting shagged on the TV. It actually took ages. They were so engrossed in the computer that they simply didn't realise what was happening. Our little joke had got weird then, because without their realisation it was simply two blokes in their twenties sat on a sofa, drink in hand, watching German porn at two in the afternoon. That's never a situation you want to find yourself in.

In the end we snapped. "Wow that's amazing! Hahahahaha!"

All the other guys turned around expecting to see something to make them go "Wow!" Instead they turned around just in time to see a heavy-set guy with a moustache finishing off.

"Awww, what the fuck?!"

Turl and I were falling about laughing. It had taken what felt like a lifetime to get them to notice, but it was worth it for the sheer timing of it. We really couldn't have planned it better if we'd tried!

What you find with guys in their twenties is, once sex becomes the subject of conversation, or thought, everything else pretty much fades into the background for an undetermined period of time.

Once this period of time had passed, we all carried on drinking, chatting and generally just pissing about for an hour or so. The porn stayed on in the background. None of us was paying attention to it. We'd all been teenagers, so had all seen as much porn as anyone really needs to see in an entire lifetime. Kev, on the other hand, seemed completed absorbed in it. His eyes didn't leave the screen for the entire time. We'd all noticed he was totally getting into it, but I figured it was funny and let him get on with it.

He'd probably take an extra-long shower before we went out, but as long as I wasn't the one in directly after him, I wasn't bothered.

Then, out of Ollie's mouth came a string of words I wasn't prepared for:

"Kev, mate, have a wank or something – it's my birthday."

We all looked at each other. Taffy said he'd had enough and walked downstairs. But sure enough, Kev whipped out his cock and started masturbating. We were all a bit pissed by this point, but we weren't *that* pissed! I mean, we were blokes and we'd been naked around each other before – but this was a whole a different level. I figured he'd put it away in a minute and we'd all have a good laugh. But no, it became a full-on SAS-style exercise. Turlough got up, grabbed the video camera and started filming. He tried to wire it up through Tim's TV but it wasn't compatible. So instead, they turned off the football game and put the porn DVD in the PlayStation, and wired up the video camera to Lance's TV in the far corner.

That computer football tournament had gone on for ages but was immediately switched off, without saving, in the name of sexual exploration (if you want to call it that; I don't know what I want to call it).

I'm still rooted to the seat at this point. Taffy has come back upstairs and is now stood in the corner with his head in his hands. Tim is laughing hysterically. Turlough is now filming close up and Ollie is chanting: "Cum! Cum! Cum!" at the top of his voice.

Now, picture the scene: I'm sat on a sofa, Snakebite in hand, and in front of me is our mate, Kev, having a wank. One TV has porn on it, and the other now has whatever Turlough is filming, which, at that point, was a close-up of Kev's penis. It's not a situation I'd ever been in before and certainly not one I've been in since.

Kev looked up at me and said, "Why are you watching?"

"I haven't got a lot of fucking choice, Kev! You've got your knob out and it's on fucking TV!"

Ollie's chants got louder and louder, and now Turlough was joining in. Tim had by now got a bit freaked out and had joined me on the sofa. He turned to me and said, "It's all a bit weird, isn't it?"

"Yep, just a little bit."

Then the point came. Kev was watching the porn, turned, had a quick glance at himself, then back to the porn. Boom! He blew his load all over his own belly. In a roomful of blokes. Not just any blokes either, but his mates.

I don't know what we were thinking but a massive roar went up in the room. "Yeeeeeaaaahhhhh!" There was cheering and high-fiving. Not with Kev, obviously – we knew where his hand had been.

"You guys are fucked up!" laughed Taff as he walked back downstairs.

What's weirder though was just how quickly the room went back to normal. Tim reloaded Pro Evolution Soccer as Kev went to clean himself up.

All of us carried on drinking and avoiding the subject, apart from the odd bit of eye contact between me and Turlough and the odd shake of the head. Were we the most mentally deranged bunch of blokes around? It kind of felt like it. You think it, don't you? I don't blame you.

Just then, Taff came back upstairs. "Gary has phoned. He's on his way round for a band meeting."

Gary was our manager. A lovely bloke, but he seemed to have the knack of picking the worst possible time for band meetings. Mind you, saying that, it was probably about five in the evening. I doubt he'd expect us all to be this drunk and having just filmed our mate wanking in the living room.

Gary only lived a couple of miles away, so he arrived pretty sharpish. We were all sat in the living room trying to act as sober as possible. We hid all the beer cans and cider bottles down the side of the sofa.

"Happy birthday, Ollie. I thought you lads would be having a few beers by now?"

"Maybe later on."

We all tried really hard to act as serious as we could. It was quite an important chat we needed to have about a future recording project. But, as I'm sure you know, the harder you try and act sober, the less sober you appear. Turlough was struggling more than anyone. I could see him looking at the video camera which was still wired up to the TV. Back in those days it was normally me that would have been the first to do this, but I was trying to hold it together. I hadn't quite hit the "silly" stage of drunk yet. It would happen, but I wasn't there yet.

I could see his finger hovering over the rewind button. He clicked it and the video camera starting making this loud motor-like sound. Gary was in the middle of imparting an important piece of information and was clearly annoyed that he'd been interrupted by some weird rewinding noise.

"What's *that?*" he snapped.

"Sorry Gary, just knocked the camera by mistake."

Gary ignored it and carried on talking. I could see that Turlough was preparing to hit "play". I just looked at him, and once I got eye contact I mouthed: "D-O-N-'T", but with a massive grin on my face. You know the way that when a kid's being cheeky, and, while they're doing something naughty, you can't not laugh? Well, that's what this was like.

Turlough hit "play" and all of a sudden the screen was alight with the chaotic scene from just a couple of hours earlier. There was Kev, wanking – with Ollie, out of shot, chanting "Cum! Cum! Cum!"

Gary caught one glimpse of the screen and he'd had enough. He threw his arms in the air in disgust before walking towards the stairs. Now I don't know what possessed me to shout after him, and I certainly don't know what possessed me to shout what I did.

"Gary. Don't go, mate. You haven't seen the best bit."

The *best* bit?! Why on earth was I shouting *that*? But then as Gary swung around, in the same way the timing had worked with the other lads earlier, he witnessed the money shot. The final scene. Cue credits.

"You fucking lads," he laughed, before stomping off downstairs.

Although Gary was probably pretty pissed off that he'd not managed to get his point across, or get the important information relayed to his band, he also knew that our bizarre behaviour and general troublemaking was the very reason people were coming to our shows, and why people were talking about us. We weren't a dime-a-dozen, skinny-jean-wearing, fashion-conscious bunch of prima donnas – we were just a bunch of punk rock kids from a small island. I think people appreciated that. I like to think so anyway. They probably just thought we were weirdos. They'd be right, I suppose. After all, this was a band that turned up to a show in Kilburn in North West London pissed on Snakebite and wearing body-warmers while the bass player held a wooden oar from a rowing boat.

After a few more beers and some burnt cheese on toast, we booked a cab and headed into Kingston. Kingston is just one big pub crawl. No matter what day of the week, it's heaving with people all out for a laugh. You get the odd dickhead like you do in any town, but here they seemed to be down to a minimum.

We'd default to the usual drinking games and general silliness that goes with any bunch of young guys on a birthday night out. An all-time favourite of ours was the running high-five. Now when we were growing up in the 80s, high fives were all the rage, but they'd kind of died out. It became our mission to get people high-fiving again. Get that beautiful feeling of a man-on-man hand-slap back into circulation!

So, when going between bars we'd run at random strangers shouting, "Come on son, hit me! Give me some skin." Some odd weirdo would clench a fist before realising we were being friendly, and some guys would act cool and ignore us, only for their girlfriends to

laugh and get involved with the high fives, thus making the

boyfriend look like a bit of a wanker – which was always funny. But in the main, people just loved it and high fived. Then, a couple of hours later you'd see the same people in another bar and they be high- fiving people. Spreading love is a wonderful feeling, and back then we were the Oliver Reed of love-spreading.

After a string of pubs, sambucas and elevated hand-slaps, we arrived at our destination. It was a massive club called "Oceania". It wasn't great but it was on three floors so at least one of the floors would be playing something that resembled decent music, and it was a reasonable £2 a pint. For the Isle of Wight, that would be cheap; but for the London area, that was practically handing out free lottery tickets.

So, there we were in the queue. We'd stood there for about half an hour or so, which was annoying, but it gave us time to look more sober for when we faced the bouncers. The bouncers in this place saw themselves as God. No-one was above them. Their steroid-induced decision was final. We finally reached the door and the bouncer points at Kev and says, "What's *that?*" I thought that was a bit harsh, but he wasn't referring to Kev as a person – he was referring to the fact that he was wearing football trainers, tracksuit bottoms and a shirt. "He can't come in like that!"

How had none of us noticed what Kev was wearing?! I think we must have all got so accustomed to his daily appearance that we were just oblivious to it. It's how he felt comfortable, so fair play; but as far as nightclub-owners are concerned, they won't have it. Smart shoes and trousers were a prerequisite, unfortunately.

So here we are in the middle of Kingston in November, freezing cold with nowhere to go. There was no point going back to get changed because that was just another cab fare, and by the time we got back to the club it would have been full anyway. Plus, to be honest, it was Ollie's birthday and as long as we were all having a laugh together, that's all that mattered.

I called a friend of mine that lived in the area and she suggested a club called "Bacchus". It was more our scene as it was an underground club that played punk music until 3 am. The whole idea of punk rock is freedom of expression so, in theory, we'd be pretty safe getting Kev in there with his football shirt on.

We stomped across town and found the club. It was in a tiny, dark back street just off the main road. If I was going to describe the area, I'd say think Jack the Ripper. You almost expected a copper with a whistle and a gas lantern to appear around the corner at any moment. We got to meet a few coppers later, but they weren't carrying lanterns.

We piled downstairs into Bacchus. It was amazing! The music was quality and the dance floor was rammed.

With anything vaguely "alternative", you always get the people who try too hard to be different. You know the ones – they dedicated their whole lives to showing the world

that they're "themselves", while actually being anything but. Well, there were a few of that sort, but mainly it was just regular folk into punk rock and booze.

As soon as we got to the bar, out came the shots. We were drinking in celebration of Kev's dress sense, because without it we'd have been in some over-sized modern place full of slags and fighters, and instead we were in a proper rock 'n' roll dive.

The load of us danced for hours to everything you can imagine. All the old classics came out: Green Day, Nirvana, Stone Temple Pilots, Pearl Jam, Blind Melon ... basically, our entire teenage years all recreated in one drunken night. The only thing I was missing was greasy, shoulder-length, bleached-blond hair. Man, I was a cool teenager.

The problem with having such a good time is that when you let yourself go, it can often lead to chaos. Some chaos was caused by me, and some by Kev. But whoever was to blame, we managed to get ourselves into a double whammy of trouble.

My mistake was simple. I saw a young lad breakdancing and I thought: I can't breakdance, but it would be *hilarious* if I challenge the guy to a dance-off. I'm not really sure what I was thinking. Maybe in my drunken state I thought everyone would laugh hysterically, the lad would become my new best friend, they'd carry me out of the building on a throne and I'd have my own Channel 4 comedy series commissioned that evening. That's how you think, or rather you *don't* think, when you're drunk. Or is that just me?

Normally, with anyone else it would have been at least a little bit funny. But this lad didn't have a sense of humour. He went first and did his fancy dancing. To be fair, he was pretty good and was trying real hard, too, which made my piss-taking attempt all the more offensive to him. His girlfriend was watching him pull his moves as I'm sure she did every time they went out – even if it was for a romantic meal, I bet a few head spins were displayed before the main course.

Then it was my turn. I can't even recall my moves but they were pretty much the same as David Brent's dance moves in *The Office*. Add a bit of 80s-style Dirty Dancing seduction and a roly poly to finish and you had my effort.

Then I pointed at the guy and said, "That's how you groove Isle-of-Wight-style, my brother," before crossing my arms in some weird rapper stance.

I've never seen a less amused face. His girlfriend, on the other hand, thought it was highly amusing, which, in turn, wound the lad up more. I think he probably thought it was going to be a massive epic dance-off that would define his dancing career. He'd tell David Letterman about this moment. I actually felt bad.

So, when you're a bit drunk and you feel bad because you've upset another bloke, what do you do? It's obvious, isn't it? You offer him a massage. Only in my case, you don't

offer, you just go right ahead and start performing on his shoulders and neck while whispering sweetly in his ear, "Oh, you are tense. Let me loosen that for you."

I don't really need to explain what happened next. There were bouncers involved, punches were thrown, and I somehow flew on my back across the dance floor and into a wall, before I was dragged off back to the bar. Tim was like, "What did you do that for?"

"I dunno. He looked tense."

The dancer and his mates all left and we lads went back to dancing, stumbling and occasionally falling over – all apart from Taffy and Kev. Taffy was being an adult, but mostly he was just keeping an eye on us. He really did play Dad on tour and he often saw us getting into trouble before we actually did. He'd then step in and save the day. He'd missed the dance-off incident so was probably beating himself up about not being vigilant enough.

Kev, on the other hand, was about to make his fatal error. And his would far, far outweigh my little 8-Mile-style dance-floor tiff.

Kev was a pretty slight guy. When he wasn't with us lot, he didn't really drink that much. And when he *was* with us, he'd just stick to beer and be fine. Well, let's be honest, this hadn't been the most normal of days. About 12 hours earlier, he'd been knocking one out while we sat and drank Snakebites and watched him on TV. I guess that would make you want to get a few drinks down your neck.

So, Kev orders some absinthe. That stuff will take the paint off the walls, the lining off your stomach and pretty much remove any sense of rationality from your brain.

Taffy had foreseen this particular iceberg and dragged Kev outside before he lost the plot in the club. I think that after the dance-off, our group was on pretty thin ice with the bouncers as it was. So Taffy and Kev went outside, and we carried on dancing for a bit.

My mate, Katy, arrived and offered a couple of us a lift home. We'd managed to get a minibus out to Kingston, but the chances were we'd have to pay for two cabs to get back. Turlough and I jumped at the chance. We'd avoid the taxi fare and wouldn't have to deal with a rather drunk Kev in the cab on the way back. Plus, to be honest, Katy was a beautiful blonde. Who wouldn't want a lift home with a beautiful blonde?

Everyone was tired and hungry, so we grabbed our jackets and left. A night out in England isn't complete without a kebab. That's just a rule or something. Although I doubt Katy was too happy about having two drunken kebab-wielding men in her car.

But when we got up the stairs and to the front of the venue, all hell was breaking loose. There were a couple of people on the floor scuffling, and the police were running over. When we looked closer, it was Taffy and Kev. Kev was going absolutely mental. He was kicking and screaming and basically going nuts. Taffy was holding him down and trying to stop him from lashing out.

The police were shouting to calm him down. We were like, "He's with us, we're all right, we're mates." But the police wouldn't have it. They kept shouting at Kev to calm down. It clearly wasn't going to work as he really wasn't thinking straight. Plus, I've never understood the police technique of attempting to subdue someone by shouting aggressively. It just seems backward.

"That's it – if you don't calm him down, we're going to arrest him."

That's all we'd need. The last thing any of us wanted was to have to deal with Kev or any one of us getting arrested. I was still on a five-year reprimand for some stupid criminal- damage charge from my youth. I didn't really need any more trouble.

So Turlough clambered into the fray, grabbed Kev's head and smashed it to the floor. Kev was instantly dazed and calmed. I'm not surprised, though; Turlough was a big lad and Kev was probably now only semi-conscious. Then (this bit made me laugh), Turlough turns to the main copper and says, "He's calm now, okay?"

The copper says, "Okay, mate. Cheers." And they all walk off.

Is that in the Metropolitan Police handbook? Rule 1) Head caving-in is fine as long as you don't wake the neighbours. Absolutely insane!

Taffy, Tim, Kev and Ollie all went off to the taxi rank and headed back to Lance's. Turlough and I had our hearts set on kebabs. Once your heart it set on doner meat, there really is no turning back. To deny it would be like losing a wife of 25 years to your best mate. I simply couldn't entertain the idea. So, poor Katy trundled along with us to find some grease-peddling Turks.

There was no way, with the amount of mayonnaise that Turlough had on that kebab, that Katy was letting us get into her car. So we stood in the street, freezing, while trying to shovel the kebab down as quickly as possible. I'm normally a fast eater, and Turlough and I would often have races at the dinner table. But we were struggling. And once the hiccups kicked in, we were done for. Rest of the kebab in the bin, and off home.

Once we arrived back, we thanked Katy for the ride and headed upstairs. There was a creepy silence. There was no way we could have beaten them back – we'd stopped for food. We walked upstairs, and there sat in only the light of late-night TV was Tim and Ollie. Kev was fast asleep on the floor.

I was like, "Has someone died or something?"

"Taffy's cleared off," replied Tim. Cleared off where?

"Dunno."

It must have been 4 am or something by this time, so goodness knows where Taffy could have got to. And why was he so bothered by a little scrap anyway? Then Tim said that apparently, before we'd got outside, it had really badly kicked off between Taffy and Kev, and had got quite nasty. Oh, dear. I'm sure he'll get over it, I thought. Plus, he didn't know anyone round here so it should only be a matter of time before he came back to Lance's flat.

I sat there with the guys for a bit trying to call Taffy and make sure he was okay. No answer. We actually started to get quite worried. He was a grown man, but that wasn't the point. We didn't know this area. He could have just wandered off in the middle of a freezing November night and got lost somewhere. So we just kept trying and trying. But still there was no answer.

After a while, we went down to the kitchen to make some tea for everyone. As the kettle was boiling, we could hear this weird noise. But because of the kettle, we couldn't make out where the noise was coming from.

"What the fuck is that?"

Now I like to pretend I'm "the big lad", but, to be honest, noises in the night scare the living shit out of me. So I started to edge toward the door. Still we could hear this eerie sound. I can't really describe it that well. It sounded vaguely like a child quietly sobbing and sniffling. I'm not that great with the idea of ghosts; and I'm certainly not that great with the idea of the ghost of a kid. But what I really didn't like was the idea that there might actually be a lost, sniffling child hiding somewhere behind the fridge. I'm not sure where laws and stuff come into play when it comes to drunken men and crying kids in the middle of the night. I'm guessing it's frowned upon.

The kettle came to its climax (as Kev had the previous afternoon) and quietened down. Now we could hear the odd sound more clearly. It was definitely someone crying and it was definitely coming from behind the fridge. So, all together we slowly crept towards that corner of the kitchen – all of us with an overwhelming desire to find out what the hell was going on, but all of us totally bricking it at the same time. We'd seen enough films to know that this sound was probably a faceless teenage girl that would then go on to massacre us and put our heads up on giant poles around the local park. That's just how these things tend to play out.

So one by one we popped our heads around the edge of the fridge. There was Taffy. Curled up in a ball in the corner, bawling his eyes out.

"Jesus, Taffy. What's going on?"

There is something heartbreaking about seeing a grown man cry. Now although we were all in our twenties and, therefore, would be classed as adults, we never saw ourselves as such. We cried all the time. Well, me and Turlough anyway. But we are a pair of emotional wrecks who cry at Macaulay Culkin films. Taffy was a 40-odd-year-old, ex-Army father-of-three. He was a real man. Men like him didn't cry. Taff was meant to be the rock for us bunch of pansies. It was really moving to see him like that.

"Taffy? Are you okay, mate? We thought you'd done a runner?"

Taff didn't say anything. He just kept his head hidden behind his hands. He was obviously ashamed to be crying in front of us. I didn't see his crying as a weakness though. None of us did. We were pretty honoured that this guy felt close enough to us bare his soul like that.

Turlough and I hadn't made the journey back with everyone else though, so, while we loved the closeness of baring souls, we were pretty lost as to why the bloody hell it had all come down to a 40-odd-year-old bloke sniffling in the corner of the kitchen. There were certainly some blanks that needed filling in. Obviously we knew that Taff and Kev had had a bit of a scuffle, but that still didn't really explain the tears. But if Taffy didn't fancy sharing, that was fair enough.

Then, as we were about to leave him be, he started talking. These words are some of the most bizarre words I've ever heard come out of another human being's mouth. So weird, in fact, that years later when Taffy got married, Tim and I recreated this moment in the best man's speech. Now, when I tell you these words, you'll understand the look of terror on some of the faces at that wedding breakfast, especially from his wife's side of the family.

"I had him by the throat!"

There was a slight pause as he wiped his eyes and composed himself.

"I was killing him!" Again, Taffy paused, breathed in deeply, and continued ...

"AND I ENJOYED IT!!"

How on earth do you respond to that? We didn't. Turlough and I took one look at each other and walked back upstairs. We were no longer bothered about a nice warm cup of tea – this day had just taken a step up from being a bit odd to downright mental. My mind at that time of the morning wasn't quite prepared to try to evaluate the previous day and night that we'd just had. The masturbating, the home-made porn film, the fighting, the breakdancing and the sobbing Welshman would all have to be evaluated the following day. It was bedtime.

A few hours later, Taffy woke us all up with a five-spice-and-garlic-clove-infused fry-up and a pack of Coke. Normal service had been resumed. Nothing needed to be said.

"Fancy the pub this afternoon?" "Sure."

10: HEADBANGERS' BALL

Isle of Wight Festival, Newport, Isle of Wight, 2006

Band members:
Gareth Icke - Vocals/Guitar
Tim Pritchard - Guitar
Turlough Ducie - Drums
Tom Ladds - Bass
Taffy - Roadie/Driver

I've waffled on about being from the Isle of Wight, haven't I? Have you ever been? You'd love it. No, really, you would. As a visitor, it's great. It's just when you get stuck in the rut that it takes its toll.

It used to be kind of famous once, though – in musical circles, anyway.

The Isle of Wight was put on the world map back in the late 1960s by the arrival of the Isle of Wight Festival. Artists like The Doors, Bob Dylan, Jimi Hendrix and Free drew an estimated 150,000 people to the Island. That's a shitload of people given that not even that many people inhabit the Island anyway.

I must explain – we all call it "The Island". You know, as if there was no other. It's a local thing.

With the sudden influx of mainland people came drugs and free love and all that other bullshit that went with the 60s and 70s. And although they cancelled the festival after just a few years, the drugs and free loving continued to take over the Island. It would explain the teenage pregnancies, heroin addicts and STD-infested skanks that now call the place their home.

That's pretty much what our Island is these days. And maybe that explains why we lads spent so much time in pubs, plotting our escape. There is nothing on the Isle of Wight for young people to do.

No great opportunities and no great hope. I suppose that's why they all get off their faces on drugs and shag each other.

That almost inevitable future was one that my bandmates and I had simply said No to. Sometimes in life, things can be that simple. It's a choice you make whether you accept your fate or not. We weren't going to. And that was the reason the band was born in the first place, to be honest. It was our ticket to a different, more exciting and less generic

life. The stardom and riches weren't the point. Our riches would come in the form of life experience; something to tell our grandchildren. In fact, most of our desires came from a TV advert! Which is sad, I know, but true. I can't even remember what the advert was for so the advertising can't have been that great. But the underlying concept had stuck with us.

Basically, a fellah is sat on a bench in a busy street. Above him are two blokes moving a piano into an upstairs window. Suddenly, the cable snaps and the guy looks up to see the piano crashing down towards him. Then the scene freezes and it flashes to all the things the guy has done in his life. Parties, trips around the world and stuff like that. It goes back to the paused scene and the Grim Reaper is fast asleep on the bench. The bloke gets up and creeps off. The slogan was something like: "When your life flashes before your eyes, make sure there's a lot to see." What a great slogan! That was our complete outlook on life from that point onwards. And that obviously meant escaping from "The Island".

We never turned our back on the place, but we didn't really play at home that often. There was nothing in it for us and no great achievement in playing to people you knew and saw on a regular basis. We'd decided that we'd play a homecoming show at the end of each tour. That meant playing on the Island about once every couple of months or so. That worked perfectly as we weren't away long enough to be forgotten, but we weren't playing so often that we'd become boring.

The other reason was that since Dan Damage had passed away and the Royal Squadron had ceased to be a venue, the Isle of Wight music scene had gone to the dogs. The younger generations simply weren't like us. And I know that makes me sound old and like a miserable bloke spouting on about how special the 1960s were.

"The youth don't know how easy they have it."

I used to hear that when I was growing up, so I'm not being like that. But what I mean is, when we were 16 or 17 we looked up to passionate musicians that did it for the right reasons. They believed in something, and their passion and dedication rubbed off on us. The younger generations didn't have the likes of Kurt Cobain and Eddie Vedder. All they were aspiring to be was famous and cool. That's the very worst possible reason to pick up a guitar. And so when they came along, and without Dan Damage to put them in their place, the scene died.

Venues stopped being venues and what little gigs there were, were supported by smaller audiences. That was unless you were playing covers of Mustang Sally and crap like that. Then the older folks would turn up in their droves to lap it up. Idiots like that couldn't give a toss about supporting anything original and so audience members were at a premium; hence why it was in our best interests to play a bigger show, less often.

So, that was our plan – a handful of hometown gigs a year and the rest of our shows would be anywhere and everywhere else.

The days of the Isle of Wight being a musical Mecca were dead and gone. The 1970's superstars were a distant memory. There was hardly any sign that a festival of that magnitude had even graced the place – apart from the odd item making the local paper because some wealthy American had spent a fortune on some Hendrix festival memorabilia from eBay; and the fact that John Peel had come to the Island to report on a potential music-scene revival in the mid-90s (which would soon go the same way). The Isle of Wight and music were now separated. Two individuals that had flirted once, but had never made it work.

In 2002, the decision was made to re-launch the Isle of Wight Festival on a smaller scale. It grew gradually, and now, as I'm sure you know, it's massive again. It's not at the level of 150,000 people, but that's more down to "health & safety" than to lack of interest. All the massive bands have been here now: Coldplay, REM, The Who, The Stereophonics, The Rolling Stones ... You name them, we've probably had them.

When they tried to sell the Festival to the local people, there were lots of promises made about what it would do for the local economy and stuff like that. Small-town people are often stuck in their ways and any idea of change is met with resistance and folded arms.

The other thing that goes against anything new is that a fair few people move to Isle of Wight to retire. They've lived their lives in the big cities and now just want to relax. I get that, but they have to understand that there are young people living there too. And in all honesty, the more things there are for the youth to be involved in, the less likely they are of turning to crime. Tragic, but true.

Now, I have no idea what the Festival has done for the local economy. Probably not a lot, as in my experience a few people cream off the top of everything and leave very little for us peasants below. Maybe that sounds a little cynical, but show me anywhere on the planet where that isn't the case and perhaps I'll change my view. But, I fear you'll be searching for some time.

The other thing that the Festival organisers did to humour the locals was to get local acts to perform on different stages across the Festival site. We, and a handful of other local bands, were absolutely stoked. What an awesome opportunity to play at such a massive event. The exposure would be incredible. At that time, there were about five or six bands that were getting out and about and trying to get their music heard and on to the next level. As I've mentioned before, we'd been all over the country, we'd been out to America and we'd been played on national radio. As far as we were concerned, we were a shoe-in for one of those slots.

As soon as the Festival came, so did the idea of fame and stardom. Everyone went out and bought a guitar and everyone thought they were a musician. All these bands popped up all over the Island. And don't get me wrong – it was great that the scene might actually start to build again, but what these bands did was nothing original. They basically got their rich parents to buy whatever guitar the current superstar was playing and then they'd set about imitating the trend of the moment. All these bands walked on to the Isle of Wight Festival bill and we hard-working bands that actually toured, were overlooked.

Needless to say, we were fuming. People even called up the local radio station to complain about what was going on. But, at the end of the day, there was nothing we could do. So every year, in the second week of June we made sure we were touring as far away from the Island as possible. I'm sure it sounds like we were bitter, and maybe in a way we were. But we'd earned the right to play at the Festival. Or at least we believed we had. And that's all we ever asked for – a fair crack at something we'd worked hard at to achieve.

So, for a few years we were overlooked and we got on with it. Then, in 2006, we were invited to play two separate slots. They'd launched a stage called "The Bandstand", and it was exactly as you'd imagine. It was made to look like an old Victorian bandstand – the kind you'd find covered in graffiti in Clapham Common, London. A load of local acts got slots and we were stoked to be involved.

On the Thursday, the site was opened up for the campers only. There were probably about 20,000 of them, but because the main stage wasn't open they'd all be in and around the smaller stages. We were main support on The Bandstand on the Thursday night, and then I was given a solo acoustic slot on the Saturday afternoon. At last – we'd landed! We could add the Isle of Wight Festival to our list of stories for the grandchildren.

"See, Grandad Gareth wasn't always such an old fart."

We rehearsed like mad for hours on end. You never knew who was going to be in the audience at something like this. We could tour for a month and not play to as many people as we were going to face in one evening.

So, when the night came we were prepared and ready to go. The Bandstand was absolutely crammed with people – Christ knows how many. Maths has never been my strong point but, take my word for it, there were a lot!

The band on before us had been a pretty chilled-out acoustic set-up so we figured we'd go for the polar opposite. Nearly all the campers would be from the mainland so they'd have no idea who we were. The plan was to walk out there like we belonged, and smash out a set as loud and as energetic as possible. Sod the nerves, we'd earned this chance and we wanted that audience to walk away from that stage with the name "Kody" firmly ingrained in their heads.

The show was going great. The crowd was lapping it up and everything was clicking into place. Sometimes you have shows like that. You can do the same things another night and it simply won't work; but on this night we were on fire. The songs sounded great, the energy was high and the onstage banter was really working as well. We used to get told off in those days for cracking jokes on stage. I remember one manager saying, "People have come to see musicians, not a stand-up."

I didn't agree with that. Our idea was to take our music seriously – but not ourselves. The songs were written about real subjects and sung and performed with the raw emotion in which they were written. But you have to have fun as well; otherwise people just want to cut their wrists. Plus, people don't like being preached to. No-one likes to feel like they're at school when they're watching a punk rock band. So in our minds, fuck the manager – we're having a laugh.

Now, our sense of humour was a little close to the bone at times and it could backfire in the smaller venues. I remember being called "sick" in Oxford once because of a joke I told.

"What's got three legs and lives on a farm...?" "... The McCartneys."

Paul McCartney's then-wife only had one leg and I thought it was a funny joke; but, apparently, not everybody did.

But anyway, with an audience the size of this festival, we'd be safe. The law of averages suggested some people would find our humour funny; and as long as some people laughed, that would make it okay. And that was how it went. A couple of belting tunes slammed together, a joke and a bit of banter and then back to the rocking out. The stage was perfect because of its shape. Bandstands are completely round and so we were completely surrounded by people. When I was singing I'd be confined to the microphone, but at all other times Tim and I would be flying around the stage, hanging over the barrier and just generally rocking out. It honestly felt like we'd made it.

I remember there was a very attractive blonde girl who'd taken up her place directly in front of me. I could only see her head as the Bandstand was about four or five feet off the ground, but it was a nice head all the same and I kept getting eye contact. I'm not going to lie – it feels pretty good to the ego when someone takes a shine to you. I was in a relationship so I was never one for the old groupie thing, but, nonetheless, a self- esteem massage was always nice.

About halfway through the set, Tim was telling one of his many jokes and the blonde girl gestured for me to come closer. So I went down on my knees and leaned down towards her. I just assumed I was going to get a request for a song or something but instead she planted one straight on my lips. It got a massive cheer and, despite me pulling away

immediately, the cheer of the crowd still managed to ruin Tim's story. I'd have a great time explaining that to the Mrs, but in the eyes of the audience it was pretty cool.

The headline band was late and so Dave, the Bandstand's organiser, had asked us to play an extra song or two. We had about a million, and any extra time we could get lapping up this atmosphere was fine by us. I'd just written a song the day before called *London, England*. It actually went on to be a single, but at that time it was brand new and the rest of the band hadn't learned it. Tim suggested I play it solo as it would create a nice vibe and allow them to run off and empty themselves of all the beer they were filling up on.

So here I was – just me and my guitar, shitloads of people and a brand new song. I liked to think I didn't get nervous but this was one of those times when it really hit me. It was just me and them. No bandmates to hide behind now. And so I cracked into the song. It was all going well for about two minutes until I noticed a flash of blonde out of the corner of my eye. Shit! The blonde girl from earlier was clambering up onto the stage. What was she going to do once she was up there? It wasn't like it was a big, loud song that you could dance to and then leap off in a giant stage dive. It was really mellow and quite moody. I sung my line and pulled away from the mic. She then appeared directly in front of me. She was actually pretty tall as her eyes were almost at the same level as mine. I could hear people starting to clap and whistle in the crowd. I was still playing guitar so I figured I couldn't win. If she tried to kiss me and I let her, sure it would get a big roar – but I'd lose my girlfriend, who I actually quite liked. And if I stopped playing guitar to restrain her, the song would be over and that would no doubt kill the vibe and be met with boos.

I closed my eyes, still not knowing what to do, and as I opened them she was gone. I looked down to find her on the floor covered in a bouncer. In that split second that my eyes were closed, a security guard had flown across the stage and bundled her to the floor. I couldn't help thinking that that was over-the-top but, at the same time, the guy had saved my arse. The crowd booed, but at least the heckles weren't aimed at me. I finished the song, the lads joined me back onstage and the pretty blonde girl, looking slightly flustered, took her place back in front of the stage.

We were left with two songs to play. We were taught that you always open on your second strongest song and end on your strongest. That way you announce yourselves and then you leave the audience with a strong tune in their heads. Because I had just played a mellow song we came back in with a tune called *1981*. It was a single we'd recently released and it was a pretty epic tune in terms of how heavy it was. Plus, put next to a solo song, it would sound like the world was ending. Well, at least that was the idea anyway. So, once again we set about flying around the stage. Tim had had his little break and was now full of beans again. As the song finished, Tim leapt up in the air and slammed back down with his guitar.

CRACK!!!

The song ended, and as the crowd was roaring I stumbled over to Tim.

"Tim."

"What?"

"You just cracked my head open."

"I can't hear you."

"You cracked my head open."

"What?!"

With that I could feel the blood dripping down my forehead, and Tim's face totally dropped.

"Fuck! I've cracked your head open!"

"Yes, Tim, you have."

As he'd slammed down his guitar, the headstock of his Gibson SG had crashed directly into my forehead. Thank goodness it was right on the hairline so any scar would be hidden. Well, until I go bald of course. Then I'll have to make up some story about how it was the graze from a wayward bullet during a Las Vegas bar brawl. Actually, fuck that, guitar smashing head is even cooler.

Because we'd been jumping about, my heart was beating as fast as hell, so the blood kept flowing and flowing; and it didn't take long until members of the audience started pointing and whispering amongst themselves. The lads and I figured we could play this one of two ways. The first way was to end the set there and then. We had just played an upbeat belter and so there was no great harm in ending on that one. Or, we could carry on and play our last song. It would look pretty cool with the blood flowing but there was always a risk that I'd pass out. Sod it! It would be rock 'n' roll if I did. Let's hammer it.

So, we played the last tune and gradually the audience stepped further and further back. Every swing of my head sent another cascade of blood onto the front row. And as for the attractive blonde girl, well I kind of felt bad for her. Just 20 minutes ago she'd been on a front row kissing a lead singer, and since then she'd been bundled to the floor by a heavy-set security guard and had the aforementioned singer's blood splattered all over her.

As soon as we finished the last song, Taffy ran on and ushered me off stage. I was getting pretty dizzy and the song couldn't have lasted any longer without me hitting the deck. Taffy dragged me to the First Aid tent. It was closed. How perfect is that? That many drunken people and the First Aid tent was closed. You have to love good organisation. But in our world, if you can't do the right thing, you have a beer. I tried to get treatment

and I couldn't so I made do with a towel round the head and a pint of lager. Now that's rock 'n' roll, people.

I remember on the following Monday after the Festival had finished, Power FM radio station in Southampton was doing a show dedicated to the Isle of Wight Festival. The guy and the woman that did the morning show were asked to name their single best Festival moment. I think the guy said his was watching The Editors or someone like that. Then the woman said her single favourite moment was watching a local Isle of Wight band called Kody.

Wow! Power FM was a massive station; we really had made it now. If we got a great endorsement from them, who knows where that could lead?

"Yeah, it was great. The singer got his head smashed open by the guitarist."

Brilliant.

11: MURDER ON THE DANCE FLOOR

The White Lion, Aberdare, South Wales, 2006

```
Band members:
Gareth Icke - Vocals/Guitar
Tim Pritchard - Guitar
Turlough Ducie - Drums
Tom Ladds - Bass
Taffy - Roadie/Driver
```

Are you sitting comfortably?

It was the summer of 2006, and it was football World Cup time. England's national team was over in Germany preparing to take on the rest of the world. The country was overwhelmed with World Cup fever. You know how it is – flags in cars, and annoying horns being blown in pub beer-gardens by drunken women who didn't even like football a week ago.

All the lads (bar one) in the band were football-obsessed, and we genuinely believed it would be our year. We pretended we hadn't thought about the fact that it was 40 years since our one and only World Cup victory, and that this World Cup was hosted by Germany – the side we beat in 1966. It's all very superstitious, but deep inside we all thought about it. Fate would come into play and hand us victory.

Only one man could even entertain the absurd idea of England being defeated – our roadie, driver, and all-round tour father-figure, Taffy. He is a Welshman, and a very proud one.

Our tour van (Alison) was plastered in England flags, much to his distaste, and we were flying down the motorway towards Wales.

We were heading into Taffy's country for a week to play a show and have a small holiday up in the Brecon Beacons. The Brecon Beacons is a mountain range in South Wales; basically, the kind of area that is stunningly beautiful until your car breaks down. Then you fear you'll become the unfortunate character in a Stephen King thriller.

Taff would constantly tell us stories about where he grew up and of his time up on the Beacons. So we thought we'd put together a show in South Wales. The gig would pay enough to cover our petrol and we could head up to the mountains for a break.

Needless to say, like all road trips, this one came armed with crates and crates of beer. One thing this band could do was drink. On average, we'd be drunk twice a day. We'd get woken up early by Taffy, hit the beer all day, and then sleep it off before that night's gig. Obviously, we'd start again at the show and do the drunken bit all over again. I hope the life insurance companies aren't getting wind of this – I don't reckon I'll get covered.

By the time we'd got onto the M4, Turlough and I were fairly drunk. We were normally the annoying ones that would tend to be loud, provocative and to remove clothing. But this time we had Taffy to annoy. He'd already had enough of the England songs being sung in his ear so we figured it wouldn't take too much more to force him over the edge.

Our weapon of choice? Flaky-pastry sausage rolls. If you got a powerful headshot, these sausage rolls would literally explode. We had a few decent headshots until one cracked Taffy really hard and sent the van veering into the next lane. I'm older now, and I've learned that throwing sausage rolls at the head of a guy that is driving at 70mph is neither big nor clever.

A few miles later, Taffy pulled into a service station to calm down. I was standing behind him queuing for a coffee. His hair was almost entirely made up of bits of pastry and sausage meat. Man, we were bullies. Yet I'm laughing while I'm telling you. I'll be checking into a hotel on the Lake of Fire when I drop dead.

We behaved after our near-death experience and thought it was probably best to stop trying to kill ourselves. We were destined for rock star deaths. I've never seen a good- looking corpse dragged out of a 15-car pile-up. Mind you, I've never seen any corpse dragged out of a pile-up. Thankfully.

At the time of the World Cup, Mars, the confectionary company that produces Mars Bars, was running an advertising campaign where it changed the name of the bars temporarily to inspire optimism that England could win the tournament. It seems like a bizarre thing to remember, but as we were driving through England we'd see these giant billboards that simply said "Believe 2006". It was a quite a cool ad campaign, although it didn't make me want a Mars Bar – it just made me want England to win the World Cup.

As we crossed the border into Wales, the Mars campaign changed. The billboards now said "Believe 2010". Wales hadn't qualified for this World Cup and would have to wait another four years until they could try again. You can imagine the piss-taking that took place once we'd seen those posters! Poor Taffy.

Actually, I have to explain – I'm not painting a nice picture of us. Taffy could give as good as he got. And when England would ultimately go crashing out to Portugal, we got some serious stick!

Anyway ...

The gig was on a Sunday afternoon at a small local pub in Aberdare called The White Lion.

Aberdare is a small town destroyed by the closure of the coal mines in the 1980s. Margaret Thatcher and her merry men destroyed small mining towns like Aberdare "for a laugh" back in those days.

The English aren't normally received with open arms here, especially ones with England flags hanging from their vehicles. But Aberdare was different to us – it was Taffy's home town and as a result the locals accepted us as one of their own. If they'd witnessed the sausage roll incident, maybe we wouldn't have been so welcome.

We pulled up at the venue and set up our gear. It was the normal agreement with the landlord: play for 45 minutes, have a break, play another 45 minutes, get paid – job done. And in the meantime, we would drink copious amounts of booze and flirt with the locals. If I remember rightly, Tim was the star of the show. He was quoting Jethro jokes in a Cornish accent. Apparently folks are easily amused in the White Lion.

We started playing and the show was going great – probably due to Taff and his family. If enough people show appreciation towards a band, the rest of the audience tend to follow suit. There is a sheep mentality at most gigs. And that's not a joke about the Welsh!

We played all originals. In some bars that caused problems. Cries of, "Play Oasis!" were common at our shows. The response would normally be, "When Oasis cover us at Wembley, we'll cover them for you. OK?"

After our first 45-minute set, Tim, Turlough, Tom and Taff all headed to the bar, but I'd been holding in my need for the toilet for about the last three songs and quickly ran off to the gents. When you're trying to sing and belt out the words, it's not that easy to hold back your bladder. You don't need to know about that though.

In the toilet was an older guy who was pretty friendly. I don't normally make a point of being overly friendly in men's toilets as it can be misinterpreted. My friendliness has resulted in phone numbers being slipped into my pocket on various occasions. I think guys take a shine to my full lips. *cough.

This bloke seemed all right though, so we had a chat. He was probably around 50-odd, and was pretty skinny. He reminded me of the kind of guy you see waiting outside the pub 10 minutes before opening time; the kind of fellah who, if he had to choose between going a day without either food or booze would choose to go hungry. He was charming enough, and I'm sure that back in the day he probably had an attractive girlfriend and promised a future of sports cars and holidays on the Costa del Sol. Then the drink took over, the girlfriend cleared off with a boring-but-steady accountant and the Costa del Sol became the Costa Coffee, High Street, Swansea.

All this is complete guesswork, but we all make snap judgements and that was mine of him – rough around the edges, but no doubt a heart of gold.

I wish I could remember his name. I really should, given what happened. But for the life of me, I can't. Let's call him "Evan". It's a Welsh name so it works for me.

Evan says that he's trying to raise money for a young child in the town who needs lifesaving medical treatment. Apparently, the lad needs an operation that can only be done in the United States, and the whole town is trying to get the money together to pay for the flight as the kid's parents don't have the funds.

In my mind, that backed up my original perception of the man. He'd probably made a few mistakes in his life, not least with the now-accountant's-wife, and now he wants to make amends in whatever way he can.

"A very honourable thing to do, mate," I tell him.

Evan asked if we'd mind announcing it on stage. That way he could go round with a bucket and collect money from the already half-drunk audience. That's a normal enough request. We got that a lot at shows we played in small towns. "Can you announce the raffle?" It's not quite the rock 'n' roll dreams we'd all formed the band with, but it was our reality and we were content with it. And actually, if I'm honest, we actually preferred it to the pretentious tight-jean-wearing sorts we found ourselves playing to in London. These people were real and weren't ashamed of who they were, whereas often folks in the bigger venues and bigger cities would try hard to mask who they really were, if they even knew. In fact, if I was a shrink I'd hand out my cards at London rock venues.

I'm rambling again.

So this guy "Evan" walks off and back out into the bar area and I get back to the reason I'm actually in the toilets. Just as I've unbuttoned my fly and began peeing, another guy sidles up next to me and says, "That's bollocks". I mean, he was right – they were my bollocks, and my penis too for that matter. But it's not something you expect to hear from a stranger who appears to be watching you pee.

"Sorry?"

"What that guy just said about the sick kid. It's all bollocks. He just made it up."

Then my new pee buddy goes into great detail about how Evan is in fact "the pub liar" and is notorious for making up stories about things that aren't actually real. The locals would just tell him to shut up, but obviously I was fresh bullshit fodder from over the border.

What the hell?! Who comes up with a whole in-depth story like that? Bearing in mind, I'd toured a fair bit by this point. I'd had a fair few random conversations, but this one

took the biscuit. The nonsense conversations I experienced in the past were normally influenced by alcohol; like some drunken guy telling me for the 13th time that he used to go to the Isle of Wight when he was a kid, and then repeatedly asking the same questions like: "Has Blackgang Chine fallen into the sea yet?" I was always too polite to tell him he'd already asked me that and would simply reply, "Not yet".

But this Evan had seemed completely sober and completely normal. Well, not *completely* normal – but then who *is?*

So I ask the guy, "Why did he make it up? So he can steal the money for himself? That's pretty messed up."

But apparently, Evan is not a thief; he just makes stuff up. For what reason, no-one knows. But he makes up stories then almost immediately forgets them. In fact, according to my new pee buddy,

Evan won't remember in five minutes what he's just spent the last ten minutes telling me. How has this guy survived 50-odd years?! Surely he'd be fat and not skinny? Because he'd eat, then forgot he'd eaten and order another Chinese?

I wash my hands, and head back to get myself a much needed beer. I mean, I enjoy social interaction, but I'm not one for long toilet conversations about sick children that don't exist.

I walked over to the lads and explained that I wasn't entirely sure what had happened in the toilet but whatever it was, it was odd. Turlough then asked if I'd found a "glory hole" in the side of the cubicle. "No Turl. Not this time, mate."

I told my bandmates what had happened, or at least what I thought had happened. But to be honest, they just thought it was funny. I don't know why I got the hump so much. I think it was probably because I'd learned to trust my intuition a lot, and at first meeting I'd quite liked Evan. Hell, I'd even invented him an ex-girlfriend who now resides with an accountant. I don't do that with every bloke I meet. I suppose I was just gutted that he'd turned out to be a fraud.

I grabbed my beer and walked back to the stage. I spotted Evan chatting away to his drunken mates. They almost all fitted the same category as him. Fifty-odd, had a tough paper round, escapism through booze and no doubt promised much in youth that they never delivered in adulthood. I sound cruel, but I'd bet my left testicle I was on the money.

So I thought, hell, I'll test the bloke – part of me hoping that Evan was telling the truth after all. Maybe he just owed the other guy in the toilets some money or something? Or the other guy was the pub liar making himself out to be the honest one. Kind of like a Scooby Doo plot.

"Hey, mate. That kid you were talking about? What's his name? I don't want to get it wrong on the microphone." A pretty straightforward question, I thought. But I'd never seen a more puzzled expression in my life. It'd been about 10 or 15 minutes since our toilet chat and he had absolutely no recollection of who I was or what giant, in-depth yarn he'd just spun me.

"What kid?" he replied.

Was he serious?!?! "Umm, the sick kid that needs treatment in the USA – the one you just went into great detail telling me about?"

Still a blank expression filled his face. "You drunk, mate?" he asks me. *Me?!* Am *I* drunk? Well yeah, a little as it happens, but not in the league of the madness that is Evan. I was annoyed now.

But the show must go on, and on it went. I walked back onto the stage, planted a big smile on my face and got on with it.

Another 45 minutes of songs and the crowd is getting more and more intoxicated, and Evan and his clan are getting louder and louder, and becoming more and more irritating (to me, anyway).

The more drunk people get, the more they want to dance. That's always cool with us. Dancing is contagious. Once a couple of people have taken to the dance floor, it tells the remaining folks that it's okay to let your hair down and have a dance. Showing appreciation to a band will not, in fact, land you in some kind of trouble.

We get to the last song of the set and Tim decides that a dancing competition would be a good idea. It's not a bad shout – a few of the dancers are getting tired and some have gone all of four minutes without a drink. The dance floor is emptying, and you can't have that for your last tune. We had to keep the buggers up there – and what better way than offering free stuff?

Most people don't actually give a shit what you give them – they're just happy that they're getting something for nothing. I reckon if you offered someone a slap round the gob, they'd take it as long as they didn't need to open their wallet.

We had no prizes for the winner. We were a rock band, not a clown act at a kid's fifth birthday party. All we could muster was a T-shirt that said "Who the Fuck is Kody?" across the front. It amuses me how much middle-aged people will tell off their kids for swearing, but when they've had a drink they love swear words. They feel young and rebellious again. It's like one "F" word and you're Jimmy Dean.

Most of the room is back up dancing. The lure of a cheap creased-up T-shirt with an obscenity on the front is too much for most of these drunks to resist. But Evan is still cackling away in the corner. He's no doubt distracting himself by concocting another fabricated tale.

There was a breakdown in our last song where it just went down to a chilled-out acoustic bit. This was perfect timing. "Oi!" I yelled. "Get your arse up on the dance floor!" (Microphones are great when you have one and the other bloke doesn't.)

Evan looked totally confused as to why I was picking on him. He just kept shaking his head. But when you have a drunken audience at your disposal you can make people do most things. So the crowd shouted and bayed at him enough to make him get up. This was my revenge. He made me feel like an idiot, so I drag him up and make *him* look like an idiot. That's a fair deal, I thought. All will be forgiven, we'll have a beer at the end and everyone is happy.

It annoys me to admit, but he had some moves. Compared with me, most people have "moves" – but this bloke *really* did. Fair's fair, he was the best of the bunch.

Tim announces him as the winner and we present him with the T-shirt.

I've kind of forgiven Evan. He'd annoyed me but pulled out some moves and redeemed himself.

Can we leave it at that point? Nope.

Evan then *sells* the T-shirt to another bloke for £5. Right in front of us! This guy has some cheek!

I almost had to give him credit for having the bollocks to do that though. Evan 2 – Gareth 1.

Then ... he steps out for a cigarette ... and bang!

Heart attack.

Pavement.

Dead.

What the hell?! This stuff doesn't happen to rock bands. This happens in real, normal, nine-to-five life. We'd spent years doing our best to steer well clear of "normal life". But here it was, rearing its frighteningly ugly head.

You know when you get those situations where there is literally nothing you can say or do to make it better? Like if a mate goes, "Yeah, my cat got run over." You can sort of think on your feet and offer some consolation with something simple like, "I'm so sorry, mate. That's awful. Really sad. How you holding up?"

But then there are other ones like, "Yeah, so I went off to South Africa on honeymoon. Wife got brutally murdered and I was given AIDS." I got nothing to reply with. That's basically how this was with Evan. None of us had a clue what to say or do.

We packed up our gear as fast as any band has ever packed up gear and we got the hell out of there. I'm not even sure if we stuck around to get paid. As far as we were concerned, this drunken crowd could become a pitchfork-wielding mob at any moment.

Once in the van, the feeling of guilt was overwhelming. I felt sick to my stomach. I made the guy dance. I just thought it would be funny; I didn't realise the guy was going to hit the floor. It was just meant to be a bit of a laugh.

We all headed back to Taffy's sister's house. Gina had been kind enough to put all of us up until we headed up to the Brecon Beacons. A LOT of whisky was consumed that night, I can tell you.

We were all sat around the kitchen table, drinking. Nobody was really saying much at first. What could we say? We couldn't change anything. We couldn't take anything back, and, to be honest, it clearly would have happened sooner or later. Whether it had been picking up a parcel from the Post Office, or walking up the stairs, his heart would have given out eventually. But that didn't change the fact that it wasn't at the Post Office. It was at our show. And it was after dancing because we'd goaded him.

We all sat there drinking until the early hours. It was the only way I was ever going to get any sleep. It had been officially the weirdest day of my life. My mind was working at a million miles per hour. Had I just killed a man? What are the karmic repercussions when it comes to something like this? I'm guessing they aren't particularly great.

Gina and her husband were lovely. They spent ages telling us it wasn't our fault, and that this stuff happens in life. After enough booze, we started to believe them.

Eventually, I fell asleep – very drunk, very emotional, and very tired. It had been a weird day to top off a landfill site full of weird days.

In the early hours of the morning I awoke to see Turlough looking at me, terrified. Turlough is a big bloke; he doesn't get terrified. Well, apart from when confronted with a spider. That's a sight you need to see. It's amazing! And with the highest pitched scream you'll ever hear!

Anyway, he's just sat transfixed, staring at me with this look of fear in his eyes. I laughed. I was like, "Mate, you all right? I'm not Harold Shipman. I'm not going to kill everyone!"

"I just saw a man. Stood above your head. Had a blacked-up face. In overalls."

I'll admit that a pitch-dark room and an apparent ghostly intruder don't work too well for me.

I shot up off the sofa. "You saw what?!"

"A man. Just stood there, looking at you."

"Where is he?! What the fuck?!"

"He just disappeared."

That was my night's sleep well and truly over with. Turlough and I ended up lying in silence, neither of us wanting to be the last one left awake with old miner man, but at the same time I didn't really want to fall back to sleep and have him creeping around me. I'd seen enough death for one day.

A few hours later, Taffy's sister, Gina, came downstairs. "Sleep well, boys?"

"Not really Gina." I replied. "Apparently, there was some man stood above me while I was sleeping."

"Did he look like a miner?" she asked.

"He had a blacked-up face," said Turlough.

"Well, this place used to be a miner's house a few years ago. Passed away."

Right, so I've been in Wales for a day and already I've accidentally killed a bloke and had a dead miner stood watching me sleeping. I'm pretty sure the whole idea of this trip was to relax and unwind. You know, to recharge the batteries before we went back out on our mammoth tours again. If this was recharging the batteries, I'm taking the charger back to Argos and demanding a refund!

The next day, we loaded up the van with beer and food and headed into the Beacons.

I don't mean to sound like I work for the Tourist Board, but it really is a paradise-like place. The Brecon Beacons could almost be Canada. And it pretty much has all the landscapes of the world, except for desert. It has rolling hills, waterfalls, forests and, of course, mountains. But best of all, given our current mental state, hardly another human being for miles. I thought I should probably avoid humans for a bit. I'd probably ask one for the time and accidentally drown them in a lake.

We'd been driving for an hour or so. We had no set plan for where we were going; we just knew that we were going "up that way a bit". Taff then spotted a tiny campsite just off the road. We had the bus so didn't need to set up tents or any of that nonsense. Just pull in and park.

The owner came out to us: "It's ten pounds each. How many are there of you?" he asked.

"Five of us, mate."

"Okay, that's forty pounds then."

I love country folk.

We walked for miles and miles over the hills, kicking a football and drinking beer. The sun was blistering and we were all starting to relax and come to terms with the previous day's events. Goodness knows how far we walked but it was a fair few miles. I think we probably saw about another three people in all that time. It was great. We ended up standing underneath this giant waterfall with the wash cascading down, literally inches from our faces. Which is nice, but if we'd moved an inch forward it would have smashed us off the ledge and dragged us down to the depths from where we'd no doubt emerge lifeless days later. That's a dark thought. I was in a dark place. But it was getting lighter. Ever so slightly, anyway.

Turlough, Tim, Tom and I have all played a fair bit of football in our lives. We're English; we're raised on it! Therefore, our ability to control a football is pretty okay in standard. Taffy, on the other hand, is Welsh, and was raised on rugby. His touch on the ball was very much like you'd imagine a baby giraffes touch to be. As a result, we climbed down banks and into bushes to retrieve the ball. A LOT. In fact, we probably only actually walked about a mile in one direction, but ran, climbed and slipped about another 10 miles trying to stop the ball from rolling down the mountains.

Tim then started playing Enter the Gladiator on his phone every time Taff tried to control the ball. Despite the name of the song, Enter the Gladiator is actually the music they used to play at the circus. And it was well fitting. After hours in the blistering sun with several beers inside, there isn't anything much funnier than watching a 45-year-old Welshman trying to keep a ball from disappearing down a ravine, with Crusty the Clown music playing in the background. I still don't know why the hell Tim had that song on his phone.

We all headed back to the campsite, pretty shattered and pretty sunburned. Taffy's sister, Gina, was en route with more beer supplies. I told you we could drink a fair bit. Well, we had people delivering supplies in those days! That's quite tragic, isn't it? Oh, well.

So anyway, as I was saying, we headed back to the campsite and got some more beers on the go. It's all well and good kicking a football around all day in a friendly, "Over here, mate" kind of way, but there is a competitiveness when it comes to boys and football. So the jumpers for goalposts came out and we all started playing with some drunken element of seriousness. The ball had barely touched the ground when Taffy had flown at me like a crazed animal. I was left crumpled in a heap covered almost entirely in Welshman.

"Christ Taff! It's called a 'rugby tackle' because it's meant for use in rugby. Are we playing rugby?!"

Taffy was banned from making any challenges and was now designated goalkeeper. "Stay there and don't hurt anyone!"

As darkness was setting in and the 10-hour football marathon was wearing thin, we set up the table and chairs outside the van and planned to have some more beers, play some cards and get some sleep. None of us had slept a lot the night before – Turlough and me in particular.

I'm a novice when it comes to cards. Basic games like "Cheat" and "Shithead" I can muster. But poker and all that stuff, I don't have a clue about. The guys all wanted to play "Texas Hold'em" which, if I'm right, is a form of poker. So I asked a basic question – I thought – which was simply, "What are the rules?" Well, the argument that ensued about what the rules in fact were made me wish I'd just whacked my head under the waterfall.

"You don't have a fucking clue! I've been playing this for 20 years!"

"Yeah, well, my dad taught me and he used to play professionally." Neither of those claims was true, I'm sure.

Taffy had had enough and went to bed and left the rest of us sat outside on our camping chairs playing Texas Hold'em. God knows if we were playing the right rules because I don't have a clue about who was right in the argument.

Hours went by just drinking beers and playing a pretty boring game of poker. It was probably really exciting for everyone else but I didn't actually know what the hell was going on most of the time. We weren't gambling with money so I was happy to go all in with almost every hand and hope for the best. Won some, lost some. Couldn't tell you which ones were which though.

The rolling valleys were completely silent. Not a street lamp or house light in sight. What's surprising is that when no man-made lights are about and it's just the moon and stars providing the light, it's actually brighter. I never really understood that but it was definitely the case that night. You could see for miles across the valleys.

It must have been around 2–3 am by the time we all thought about turning in. After all, it had been a pretty tiring couple of days, both physically and mentally. We'd done well to last out that long.

Just as the four of us were packing up the table and collecting the empties, we heard a car. It must have been lower down in the next valley as we couldn't see anything, but the engine had broke the silence. It was obvious that it was coming on the same road we'd headed in on. It was the only road it could be on. Now call it a sixth sense or whatever, but none of us felt particularly comfortable about this car. There was just a weird *knowing* that something wasn't quite right. Turlough instinctively flicked off the lights from the inside of the bus and we all stood there in darkness. A few minutes later, the car's lights appeared on the horizon.

It was heading on the same road that we were parked next to. This car was going to drive straight past where we were. Now, mate, I know this sounds weird. You're thinking: "It's a car! Why were you freaking out?" And it's a good question; but unless you've been to this place, you can't picture it. You don't go for 3 am drives around these parts. It's a tiny winding country lane with sheep everywhere. It would be lethal. Plus, there were no houses around so goodness knows where they would be heading. Just go with me on this. It felt sinister.

The car came closer and all our hearts were beating double-time. It stopped about a hundred yards away and parked up on the verge. It was one of those massive four- wheel-drive vehicles with a long wheel base. I have a mate that owns a Mitsubishi pick- up truck. It was kind of like that, but more expensive-looking. Whoever owned this pick- up had a few quid in the bank. But what the hell would some rich bugger be doing up here in the middle of the night?

A couple of minutes later, four massive blokes got out. Turlough, Tim, Tom and I all hit the deck. Whatever they were doing up here, I didn't fancy our chances against them. We were boozy musicians; that's where we started and ended. I don't mind boxing on the Nintendo Wii – that doesn't hit you back.

They were stood chatting for a bit but we were too far away to hear what was being said. So we tried to get nearer. God knows why. I think we probably wanted to listen to see if they were saying, "Yeah, so there's the Kody van. Let's do 'em!" At least then we could have pegged it off somewhere. I would have headed straight for the waterfall. At least it would have been a beautiful place to die.

So, the four of us lads were now up against the fence. We were about 50 yards from the creepy vehicle and its giant occupants. I still couldn't understand a bloody word though, and being Welsh just made it worse.

They were shuffling around at the back of the truck. There seemed to be a struggle going on but with what we couldn't see properly. It looked like a big, long black bag; but in their shadows, and from that distance, most things looked black.

They disappeared into the field opposite and out of sight.

We all stayed there by the fence, perfectly still, just looking at each other. What the fuck had we just witnessed? Whatever it was, it was odd.

"Maybe they're poachers?" said Tom. "In a 25-grand truck? I doubt it!" I replied.

"Yeah, and another thing, I've never seen poachers actually arrive with their prey," added Turlough.

Then, from the field, came the sound – a sound so terrifying that I have never heard anything like it before or after this day.

A gunshot rang out across the valley – the sound echoing all around. I can still hear it now. It sent shivers down me like nothing I can describe. We all stayed rooted to the spot. Now was certainly not the time to be drawing attention to ourselves.

We all wanted to know what the hell was going on in that field, but, like I said, I wasn't going to take a stroll over there to introduce myself!

"Hello, lads! My name's Gareth. Now me and my mates over there couldn't help but notice that you've just killed something."

After what felt like an hour later (but was probably no more than 15 minutes), we saw the men coming back to their truck. They were all holding torches so we kept our heads down. The last thing we needed was for one of them to catch the reflection in our eyes – in our bloodshot, sleep deprived, *terrified eyes*. Did I mentioned we were drunk before? Yeah, this will sober you up.

Once they were back at the truck, the torches were put away and we could raise our faces again. We were then met with another terrifying realisation. The four blokes were just that – four blokes. Minus whatever the hell they'd taken into that field and shot. This was the most surreal situation I'd ever found myself in.

None of us was focused on the fact that some poor bastard had more than likely met his end in a dark, overgrown field. It sounds selfish, but it's just a natural human instinct. Our focus was purely on not being victims two, three, four and five. If they had seen us, they wouldn't have asked us to stay quiet about what had gone on. We'd have joined that lad in the killing field!

"Do you think they've seen the van?" asked Tim.

"I fucking hope not, mate. Because we're fucked if they have," replied Turlough and I, almost in unison.

The engine started up and the car's bright lights came on full beam. They shone directly at us and directly at our van. There was no bloody way they didn't know the van was there. Also, think about it ... if you see a vehicle in a busy town area in the middle of the night, it's more than likely to be empty and just parked up overnight. But this was the middle of nowhere. There was no chance that our van would be parked up without us being either in it, or at least nearby. And remember, that gunshot rang out like a firecracker; anyone within a three-mile radius would have heard it.

All this is spinning around in my mind because the car hasn't moved yet. It's still sat there, just 50 yards away with its headlights fixed firmly in our direction.

Slowly, it started to pull away, but because the roads are so narrow there's no chance it can turn around. It's got to keep going in the same direction it came from, and, therefore, would be driving right past us and our tour wagon.

As it slowly passed us I had this horrible vision of its lights waking up Taffy. He'd been asleep throughout all of this and could quite easily have woken up as the heavy car rolled towards the bus. What if he sat up and looked out of the window? That's all we'd need! And he wouldn't know any of what had gone on so would probably have waved or something!

The car kept going and, after what felt like a lifetime later, passed the bus and headed off into the distance. Any minute now I could imagine a brake light coming on. We've all seen the horror films where the killer starts to leave and the woman in the basement thinks she's safe. She's watching him leave through the cracks in the floorboards only for him to stop in his tracks, kick up the mat and discover the trap door. And we all know what happens to the woman! But no brake lights appeared and the truck vanished over the hill and into the next valley. We'd survived, for now.

We stayed glued to the spot, listening to the car's engine fade down through the next valley and then watching its lights as it climbed back up the other side, until eventually it was gone.

I've never been a fan of "the boring life", but I really didn't sign up for this. I just wanted to sing some songs and drink some beers, maybe get a bit of success, fall in love with a pretty girl and live happily ever after. I didn't realise the music business would lead to me being surrounded by death and carnage.

For the second night running, none of us – except Taffy – got any sleep. We were just fuelled by pure adrenaline. As soon as the sun came up, we were over in the field looking for some sign of what had gone on – some blood or some tracks or something. We found nothing.

Absolutely nothing.

None of us knows what happened that night. Was it poachers? Was it gangsters from Cardiff or Swansea "offing" someone that hadn't paid their drug bill on time?

We'll never know. And I'm not sure we ever really want to. I needed a pint.